VISION
of HOPE

REBUILDING A LIFE DESTROYED BY
DRUGS AND ALCOHOL

LEILANI FABER

All rights reserved. No part of this book may be reproduced or transmitted in any form or by any means, electronic or mechanical, including photocopying, recording, or by any information storage and retrieval system without express written permission from the author, except in the case of brief quotations embodied in critical reviews and certain other noncommercial uses permitted by copyright law.

Printed in the United States of America.

Brilliant Books Literary
137 Forest Park Lane Thomasville
North Carolina 27360 USA

To my wonderful children, my mother and my late father, who chose to forgive me and believe in me. They inspire me every day to be a mother, daughter and human being, deserving of their love and respect.

CONTENTS

"Unspoken Promises" i
Foreword iii
Prologue v
The Fire 1
Doc #1142212 9
Chrysalis 15
Comfortable Words 21
Love And Loss 29
Supernatural 35
Wrestling With My Demons 43
Resentments And Regrets 49
There's No Place Like Home 53
Working For A Living 59
Non-Traditional Student 65
12 Steppin' 73
Life Is Good 79
Class Dismissed 85
Epilogue 89

"UNSPOKEN PROMISES"

Here are some promises I'm willing to make
If you keep on taking the chances you take
Between you and me, they need not be spoken
But no matter what, they will not be broken

You may be a player and new to this game
If so turn and run back the same way you came
Over time you'll need much larger doses of me
You can't fathom how total your losses will be

First I'll take your desire for living life right
Your days I will twist up and turn into night
I'll take everything that you love and hold dear
I'll take all life's pleasures and leave only fear

Yes I'll take your new car and I'll take all your wealth
I'll take that great job and I'll take your good health
I promise to take all your land and your home
Then I'll take all you'd get in the way of a loan

I'll take all your treasures, your jewelry, your toys
I'll take all your children—your girls and your boys
Your friends I will take from you, one by one
Your family I'll tear apart, father from son

Leilani Faber

I'll cause you regret, wracked with guilt and with shame
I'll cause your good name to go straight down in flames
I'll bring you real misery, worry and woe
I'll bring you more trouble, oh, more than you know

I'll make you see people in bushes and trees
Look for cameras and microphones hidden in cheese
I'll cover your body with oozing red sores
As the cops come and knock in your windows and doors

I'll take your bright future; I'll revoke your bail
I'll cause you to stay in a cold lonely jail
I'll take all your weeks, your months and your years
I'll leave you with nothing…nothing but tears

When my demons get rolling, there toward the end
I'll cause you to murder your very best friend
You might be real lucky and get off as insane
But normal brain function, you'll never regain

"What is real?" you will ask, and then "What is not?"
You'll think "Maybe I'll know if I do one more shot."
So you grab a syringe (but it's really a knife)
Then I'll finish you off by taking your life

If you think that I'm lying about what I'll do
Keep doing what you're doing, you'll soon have your proof
Don't say you weren't warned; I warned you too well
I'm Meth, Ice, I'm Crystal and I'll see you in HELL!

—Revised from original, Leilani Faber, 2004

FOREWORD

In 2006, Dick Dixon and I were privileged to record the stories of 30 southwest Missouri methamphetamine addicts in sustained recovery who told us how they got on, how they got off, and how they stay off meth. We shared those in our book, *Ozark Meth: A Journey of Destruction and Deliverance*. Their accounts of normal lives gone wrong with the introduction of meth were fascinating and heart-breaking and strikingly close to anyone else's life. Leilani Faber's was one of those and now she has shared her own complete narrative in her book, *Vision of Hope*.

Leilani's book is an intimate account of a life so much like any one of the rest of ours that except "for the grace of God", any of us or one of our loved ones could find ourselves in a similar situation. The most incredible part of her story is her remarkable recovery and the extraordinary contributions she continues to make toward the recovery of so many others.

It is a common myth amongst addicts that what they do with their life and their body is strictly their own business but in simple yet poignant terms, Leilani tells us how her life in meth impacted the lives of her children, her mother, and her long term relationship with her siblings. She also speaks with great candor of overcoming the shame, guilt, anger and resentment associated

with a former life of drug abuse, a major step that many addicts never seem to embrace. This inability to complete the circle leaves them unprepared for a world that does not and probably never wil l,completelyunderstandtheirviewoflife.Leilanihasnotonly made this difficult transition, she uses that knowledge and insight every day to help others make those necessary steps to return to a productive life.

Vision of Hope is an important contribution in the growing number of stories by recovering addicts, for its well-written account in terms that are touching yet honest, in both the low points and high points of her story. Perhaps most significantly, Leilani Faber's life story brings us to a conclusion that includes a current life and an optimistic future that should make her, her children and her mother proud. It literally offers hope for anyone who has found their life severely impacted by meth or other drugs and demonstrates that despite the damage done by meth use, with hard work, redemption is possible and a new life awaits anyone willing to make that commitment.

Laura L. Valenti, co-author
Ozark Meth: A Journey of Destruction and Deliverance

PROLOGUE

After many years of promising myself and being encouraged to begin, I am finally committing to spending a portion of my time writing. I have identified myself as a writer as far back as I can remember—even when I was very small. Maybe it's because I've always loved to read. Reading gave my life so many gifts—escape, imagination, knowledge—and so many questions. But as they say, a writer is someone who writes, so if I am to truly call myself a writer, I must begin to do so.

I'm the type of person who questions everything. At this point in my life (early 50's), I've come to understand that we know what we know only until new knowledge surfaces that refutes what we know. And the cycle continues ad infinitum.

Some of my earliest questions were about the nature of reality and my own existence. When I was four or five, I remember thinking, "How do I know that anyone else really exists? I know that I exist, but maybe everyone and everything else is just a type of movie that I'm seeing in my mind's eye meant to fool me into thinking I'm not alone."

I don't know when I began to let go of this question. Maybe my brain developed some more, or I grew into the next stage of Piaget's or Freud's theory of development. I've never outgrown being highly analytical, which can be a blessing and a curse. My problem is that once I analyze something and find that it is flawed or in need of repair, I either try to fix it, or toss it aside for its imperfections.

Maybe that's where the basis of my troubled past lies. I have always found myself sorely lacking for many reasons and on many levels. I know I'm not unique in that manner as I've found that most people find themselves lacking in at least a few characteristics. It's sad, but true, that people with a healthy self-esteem are few among the young, but much more common among the older population. I think I'm getting closer to that ideal, although, I've found that forgiving myself for my addict behaviors is something I continue to struggle with.

It's been several years now since I used methamphetamine. It took me a few more years of dancing with "demon alcohol" before I realized that I couldn't handle that drug either. And it is a drug—period! Just try to talk about alcohol as anything separate or different from the category of "drug" and my daughter will set you straight in a heartbeat.

Since reuniting with me and her older brother, she has attended many Narcotics Anonymous meetings. As a matter of fact, she loves N.A. We actually developed a sort of extended family from our home group in Monett, Missouri. Monett is a little town southwest of Springfield where we lived when our reunification became official. What I mean by "reunification" is normal, unsupervised visitation. I lost custody of my daughter in 2004 and was allowed six, two-hour supervised visits per month due to my nightmarish train wreck of a life that started with just a quarter gram of meth.

In the following chapters of this book, I will attempt to tell my story of addiction and recovery. There are many more stories of my life to tell, but I need to start with this one, the most recent and the most challenging. My hope is that you will be able to understand the addict in your life (maybe yourself) and begin the healing process. I know it has been healing for me.

Even more than understanding and healing, I want you to glean hope for it is only through a vision of hope that we can begin to see a different future. As we tell the addicted offenders at the prison where I work—"Tomorrow does not have to be what yesterday was." Read on...

THE FIRE

I could start at the beginning of my addict behaviors in an attempt to explain how I got here, but instead, I'll begin with the night of June 17, 2004, the night it all ended. It was a horrific night, a night that came to represent a point in time like B.C. and A.D. We began to refer to all other events as "before the fire" and "after the fire."

It was a warm summer night in suburbia, a week night, so not much was going on. From the outside, the blue house on the south side of El Castile looked much like the other houses on the street. It was well maintained with a manicured lawn, rock-lined flowerbeds full of blooms and pruned shrubbery. In the backyard an above ground pool with a water slide coming off the deck waited patiently for laughing children to enter its chlorinated depths. In a culture that places so much emphasis on appearances, this home appeared to house a "normal" middle-class family. But as they say, "appearances can be deceiving."

At around ten o'clock that night, my fiancé got a call from his daughter. She was spending the night at a friend's house with which she had just had a fight. She wanted to come home. My children, who were six and ten, were asleep in their rooms on the main floor. Mark (my fiancé) and I were downstairs preparing to do some cooking. I was getting ready to cook the alcohol off a batch of "pseudo" while he attempted to pull the last remnants of meth from a lye bed.

We were fighting over something—I can't remember exactly what. When you are tweaking for days on end, it doesn't take much to get you in your feelings. He left without a word. Ironically, that is the last moment he remembers from his life…before the fire.

I don't remember what I did exactly while he was gone. Maybe I did a line. I'm sure I checked and rechecked the monitor for the cameras mounted on various points outside the house. I may have worked on one of my painting projects that I enjoyed doing while high. As a matter of fact, I used "smoking while cleaning paint brushes" as an explanation for the fire when asked by the fire investigator later that night.

Mark returned with his daughter sometime before midnight. After he put her to bed in the room she shared with my daughter, he came downstairs. Behind the linen closet at the end of the hall was a hidden room we had built. First we put a false wall in the walk-in closet of a bedroom we called "the jungle room." Then we removed the shelves of the linen closet and cut the sheetrock out from the floor to the bottom shelf. It was well hidden by the shelf and the wood trim that held it in place.

We had a sliding shelf that was about five feet long by eighteen inches wide inserted in this space. On it, we lined up plastic totes full of various items needed to manufacture "red and black" methamphetamine. "Red" stands for red phosphorus and "black" for black iodine.

Not everyone realizes that there are different types of meth made by different means. Mark had been using mostly red and black meth and "ice" for twenty-four years. It doesn't have as many harmful side-effects, especially the ones you see evident in the mug shots of longtime anhydrous users. He still had all of his teeth and was even a little bit overweight. Doctors at the Mercy Burn Unit said that it is probably why he survived—that and being well hydrated. He drank a lot of Gatorade and water.

It was some time after midnight on the morning of the 18th of June that it happened. I heard a crash and Mark started cursing. I walked out of the office into the hall and opened the laundry room door. What I saw stopped me dead in my tracks. Mark was almost completely covered in flames. There was also fire on the floor leading over to a laundry sorter that was placed beneath a laundry chute that I had put in.

The laundry chute was one of many of my tweaking projects, like the kids' bathroom walls painted to match the "Under the Sea" shower curtain. Some tweakers bead or play online games or do scratchers tickets. I did construction and painted. In the newspaper they described it as a laboratory ventilation system that was vented into the children's bedrooms. It was actually a laundry chute made of metal furnace piping. There was a small door upstairs at the end of the hallway where the clothes were placed. It went through my bedroom closet and came out of the wall downstairs into the laundry room. Pretty genius, I thought. But I digress.

Mark ran past me out of the room and I broke through my fear and grabbed a fire extinguisher. I pulled the pin, pointed it at the fire and pulled the trigger, but it was doing no good. Suddenly, Mark reappeared and grabbed the extinguisher from me. He was no longer on fire. I don't know if he did a "drop and roll" in the other room or what, but he took over. It still wasn't working on the fire so I ran out of the laundry room and into the office. The lower level was a few feet below ground level in the back of the house, so I went to the window and opened it. I popped off the screen, climbed out and began to unwind the hose from the reel that was located beside the window. When I had enough let out, I turned on the water and climbed back in the window, went through the office and into the laundry room.

By this time, the flames were licking at the wall and the laundry sorter had begun to burn. As I aimed the water hose, Mark once again caught fire. I later learned that Mark had placed a glass beaker with a lye bed in it on an electric burner on top of the laundry sorter. Since Mark doesn't remember, I can't say exactly what happened, but evidently the beaker cracked and the camp fuel in the beaker ignited. It must have splashed onto Mark, although that doesn't explain how he was burned over so much of his body.

As he ran from the room, I continued to try to put the fire out with the hose. It appeared to be working, but was probably just burning itself out on the concrete floor. When Mark returned once again, he walked into the room, and suddenly his head was on fire. I threw down the hose, grabbed him and pushed him into the bathroom, then the shower and turned on the water. My mother told me later that when they went back into the house they found Mark's skin all over the walls of the shower. It was pretty grotesque.

When I knew he was okay, I went back into the laundry room to assess the situation. The fire had stopped burning on the floor but was climbing up the wall into the laundry chute. I sprayed more water onto it, but it was not helping the situation. Then Mark came in and started grabbing the lab materials and placing them back into the plastic tub. He then said we should move it and the other tubs to the pool closet under the deck. I don't know in what universe that would sound like a good idea, but we were high, tired and panicking. So we pulled everything out of our secret room, shut it back up, hauled the tubs through the office window and threw them into the pool closet.

Afterward, I called 911 and asked for a fire truck and an ambulance. Mark and I then went upstairs and woke the kids up. When Mark picked up his daughter to carry her out, he flinched as her hands touched his scorched flesh. At the time, it just looked like a really bad sunburn.

With my daughter in my arms and his daughter in his, we then woke up my son who followed us out the back door, across the deck and down the steps into the yard. On our way out I realized that it was the attic fan which was right above the top of the laundry chute that was causing the flames to be drawn upward toward more flammable material. I turned it off as we walked out of the girls' room.

Once outside, the kids became very upset. My son became especially fearful when he realized that the dogs were still inside. We had a Weimaraner and a Cocker Spaniel, Bruno and Mocha. Mark went back in and got the dogs. When he came out, I told him to sit still and asked his daughter to spray him with the water hose to cool his burns while I went through the downstairs one more time looking for evidence that we may have missed. It was ridiculous looking back at it because we put everything in an easy-to-find location even leaving a trail of filters and funnels from the office window to the pool closet.

When I was satisfied that I'd cleaned up enough, I took the hose from Ali and pulled it over beneath my second floor bedroom window. I don't remember talking to Mark about what I wanted to do, but when I looked up, he was leaning out of the window. It took a couple of tries, but I was able to pass it up to him and he pulled it into the house. I ran back inside and up the stairs to Mark who was now spraying water on the fire as it leapt through the opening at the end of the hall. Now that the attic fan was off, the fire had less ferocity and was more or less contained to the flammable materials at the top of the chute which included the master bedroom closet.

I took the hose from Mark who was obviously in a lot of pain and told him to go back outside, gather the kids, and wait for the ambulance in the front yard. I'm not sure how long it took me to finish putting out the fire, but when I was satisfied that it was out, I tossed the hose out the bedroom window and went back outside to turn it off.

As I made my way to the front of the house, I heard sirens and then saw the flashing lights of an emergency vehicle. Unfortunately, it was not the ambulance that I was hoping for. In the driveway, I saw Mark doing a plank, or "frozen push up," on the concrete so that his skin didn't touch the ground. The kids were trying to put the dogs into Mark's van so they would stop barking and the emergency personnel could approach. My daughter ran up to me and I held her on my knee as a fireman came toward me.

I told him that the fire was out then I asked him where the ambulance was. He made a call requesting an ambulance and began to question me about the fire. I told him that I had put it out with a hose. He and the other firefighters then went into the house to survey the damage. They never had to pull a hose.

I took the children next door to our neighbor's house. They were new neighbors so I didn't really know them. When I saw a woman come onto her front porch, I waved at her and asked if we could come in so the children would be away from all the commotion. She was nice enough to let us in.

The children and I sat on her sofas. I was trying to get them to lie down when the woman returned with several blankets. I was barefoot and wearing shorts and a tank top so I wrapped one of the blankets around myself then tended to the kids. There was no way that they were going to fall asleep after being rudely awakened and traumatized by all the chaos.

When we heard a knock on the door, the neighbor answered it. At the door were a deputy and the fire inspector. They had a few questions for me about the fire. I told the kids I would be right back, but my daughter started crying. She calmed down when my son came over, sat by her and put his arms around her.

They took me next door and downstairs to the laundry room. They wanted me to walk them through everything that happened when the fire started through me putting it out. I explained that I wasn't in the room when it happened but I believed that Mark was cleaning paint brushes with a solvent when it started. I told him that he must have been smoking and a hot ash ignited the solvent starting the fire.

As they walked me back upstairs I was thinking how smooth I was coming up with that "off the cuff" lie. They had me sit on the couch while an officer sat on the coffee table, watching me closely. I was shivering at this point and asked if I could get a blanket. I think the deputy must have been new because he had to ask a senior officer for permission to allow me to cover up. Permission was denied and I was told that it wouldn't be much longer.

Before long the fire inspector came upstairs, told the deputy to cuff me and walked me back downstairs. In the laundry room, they asked me where the paintbrushes were. I couldn't answer that. They then asked me where the paint thinner or acetone was. I couldn't answer that either. They then led me back upstairs and sat me down on the couch. The fire investigator told me that they found the meth lab and knew there was no paintbrush cleaning going on. I was read my rights, led outside, and seated in the back seat of a Sheriff's car.

As I sat there in shock staring at the floor, an investigator came to the car, opened the door and squatted down next to me. There was a woman with him holding a clipboard. He asked me for names of relatives who could come pick up the children. I gave them the name of my ex-husband and his number. Mark's ex-wife was in a drug treatment center, so I gave them the number of her boyfriend. As the woman—I assumed a DFS worker—wrote down the information and walked away, the investigator leaned in and said, "You know Mark is going to die don't you?" "No way," I thought to myself. "When he dies," he went on, "we'll charge you with felonious murder." He then stood up and slammed the car door. I dropped my head and began to cry.

DOC #1142212

The Greene County Jail was busy that night, although I'm not sure why. It was a Thursday night, or rather, very early Friday morning on June 18th. Because they were so busy, they sat me down on a long wooden bench just outside the booking entrance.

I believe I was in shock at this time. I was cold, possibly due to my earlier firefighting activities. Lying down on the hard bench, I stared blankly at the wall across from me. After a while, an officer came for me and led me through the metal detectors into the main booking area. I remember standing at the counter as they placed several documents in front of me. They took my rings, the only personal property I had on me aside from my clothes. I know they wanted me to sign something, probably an acknowledgement that they had my effects. Instead, I lay down on the floor and curled up into the fetal position.

Someone picked me up and led me to a holding cell along the perimeter of "the pit," an area where other offenders waited to be processed. There was nothing in the cell but an elevated concrete slab with a thin, plastic covered mattress on it and a stainless steel sink/toilet combination in the corner. Large windows and a mostly glass door allowed the corrections officers to see me from most of the booking area.

I don't know how, but I managed to curl up on the concrete slab and doze a bit. I started out lying on the mattress but I was so cold that I decided to get under it creating some measure of warmth. After a few hours, I woke up and felt the urge to urinate, looked over at the toilet and realized there was no toilet paper. I got up and stood at the door with my face pressed up against the glass. Looking around the room, I tried to catch the gaze of someone who could help me. Eventually, an officer looked at me and I began to bang on the glass and look at him with pleading eyes. He approached, obviously annoyed, opened the door and asked me what I wanted. I asked him for some toilet paper and, as an after-thought, a cup so that I could get some water from the sink.

It was some time later that morning when they came and got me from the holding cell and took me to the showers. They were directly across from the holding cells on the other side of the pit. Inside a tiny room, I faced a female corrections officer behind a window. Behind me was the shower. I undressed and handed her my clothes. She had me raise my arms, open my mouth and stick out my tongue. Next was the really fun part of turning around, grabbing my ankles, squatting and coughing. I knew the drill having done it twice before.

Because I was acting a little bizarre and definitely despondent, they put me in what female offenders called a "blue party dress." This could be described as a stiff moving blanket with arm holes, a neck hole and Velcro fasteners. All offenders considered suicidal are put into one of these outfits and placed in a completely bare cell—for their own protection.

Orange plastic sandals completed the look. They usually give offenders basic necessities like a tooth brush, tooth paste and a comb. I guess they were too dangerous for me to have at that point. They then led me to the stairs that took me to my new home on the 4th floor, female unit, or "pod" as they referred to it. I was placed in an isolation cell and put on a 72-hour suicide watch.

This cell had a metal bunk bed, desk and stool, sink/toilet combination, toilet paper and 24-hour video surveillance. There was no blanket, no sheets or pillow, no socks or other warm garments that could possibly be used as a noose.

None of this really registered for me at the time. I was emotionally numb, physically drained and withdrawing from meth. All I wanted to do was sleep and never wake up. Under normal circumstances, I could never have slept in those conditions. They keep the temperature in the jail very low in order to keep the spread of illness down. So, in order to stay warm enough to sleep, I had to make my own comfort in this cold, stark place.

I laid on my side on the metal bunk, pulled my legs, arms and head into my "party dress" and refastened the Velcro straps tightly around the neck. The stiff material created a pup tent of sorts that trapped my body heat, at least enough to stop my shivering. It worked well enough to allow me to relax and drift into a deep sleep. And I slept, and slept, and slept…for three days. I got up three times a day, when they brought me my meals. I would eat everything on my plate, drink the weak cup of Kool-Aid, use the toilet and crawl back into my makeshift tent.

Early on Monday morning two men, one a corrections officer and the other a mental health professional, entered my cell. The C.O. carried a set of Greene County-green scrubs while the other carried a clipboard and a pen. The man with the clipboard asked me several questions as he scribbled down my responses. His obvious intention was to assess my propensity and intention for immediate self-harm. I don't remember exactly what I said, but it satisfied him. He instructed the C.O. to leave the scrubs, I was told to get dressed, and they left.

Shortly thereafter, a different C.O. came to my cell and led me out to the desk at the edge of the pod. I was told to place my left hand on the desk. It was then that I noticed the hospital bracelet on my wrist. On it my name and number was printed. The C.O. matched my name, number and photo to the appropriate page in a 3-ring binder. Even though I was divorced, my name within the Missouri Department of Corrections was, and remains, Leilani F. Canella, Number 1142212.

After checking me out of the pod, I was cuffed and led downstairs where I joined several other offenders in a holding room. There were several benches in rows within this room. Sitting on them were women and men, dressed alike, wearing handcuffs and, for the men, ankle cuffs as well.

The memories of my early incarceration are patchy. I don't recall the time when I was moved from the holding room to the courtroom. Over the course of the next five months, I would go through this same routine many times. After a while, they all blurred into the same memory.

The next thing from that day that stands out is a memory of sitting in a juror's chair to the left of the judge. My toes were painted a metallic blue. I remember staring down at them for a long time examining the chips and worn spots. I was too ashamed to look up and longed to return to my cell where I could escape once again into sleep.

I had been in court before, but never under these circumstances. I was extremely scared and felt like my life was over. In a way, I was right. My previous life was over and I was embarking on a new life. Just like a fetus, I would have a period of time where I would not see daylight and, for all intents and purposes, my life would not really begin until I was released.

When I heard my name called, I looked up. A public defender approached me, introduced himself, and said he was representing me. I stood up and followed him to the table in front of the judge. I heard the charges being read off, all 14 of them, and my gaze strayed downward, that shame overwhelming me once again. It wasn't the manufacturing charges that caused me the most pain. It was the three child endangerments.

I don't remember what else was said, whether my attorney offered a plea or waived my preliminary hearing. I heard someone say that my bond was $250,000. They mentioned my previous case in which the bond was raised to $250,000. The room closed in on me and it was all I could do to keep breathing.

After the hearing, my attorney led me to a small conference room just outside the courtroom. He used this time to advise me as to the enormity of my situation. Mark, he told me, had been burned over most of his body and was going to die. This was the second time somebody had made this incomprehensible statement to me.

I believe I asked if he was sure about this and his response was that Mark had a 1% chance of survival. They were planning his funeral. After I heard this devastating statistic, the rest of what he said sounded like Charlie Brown's teacher…wah, wah, wah, wah. I managed to pick out the words "felonious murder" and "25 to life."

I stayed there in my head for some time as he laid out a plan for my defense. Actually, there was no defense. He was hoping for a plea that got me closer to 15 years. This, of course, was unacceptable to me and my mind could not even go there. My thoughts turned back to Mark. "They obviously don't know Mark," I thought. He's as tough as they come. He had survived so many close calls with death, usually during drug deals gone wrong.

But he had been burned over the majority of his body and nobody his age survives and comes back from burns that bad. They said they were second and third degree burns. I'm sure that going back into the room and coming out on fire each time was the reason. What's ironic is that a few weeks before this happened we had been up all night at a fellow meth cook's house making a batch when Mark was burned over a portion of his thigh.

Early that morning he was cooking some alcohol off a last batch of pseudo in a pan and someone decided to light up a pipe with a torch. He was standing right next to Mark and the alcohol in the pan caught fire. Mark panicked and threw the pan into the sink sloshing the alcohol and fire back onto his leg. I was standing right next to him as he was frantically patting at the fire on his leg with his hands. I grabbed a towel and tried putting it out with that. When that didn't work I grabbed a glass and put some water in it and threw it on him. That did the trick.

He was in a lot of pain and I wanted to take him to the hospital. He refused, so I went across the street to Ramey's and bought a bag of ice. I came back and placed the entire bag on his leg. He wanted to take it off after a while, but I wouldn't let him. I was freaked out, but Mark seemed to take it in stride. When we went to pick up the kids later that morning, he told his ex-wife that he had been mowing and overfilled the tank, splashing gasoline onto the hot engine which ignited and burned his leg. It sounded reasonable and she bought it.

I must have returned to this incident as a reference point and decided that this was somehow comparable. I was so wrong, but it gave me hope. That's all I needed. Just a spark of hope is all it took to banish the thought of Mark dying and me spending the rest of my life in prison. I didn't have to lend it any credibility or possibility. In this mental state, maybe I could get through this. Maybe...

CHRYSALIS

"I am Healed" by Kailani Rose Faber, 2004

I am cocooned in the bright white healing light of God's love. As a chrysalis, I am recreating my entire being—releasing, repairing, reforming it anew. Soon, like the butterfly, I will emerge reborn—same body, same soul—yet transformed in essence, perfect and whole. Thank you God!

Kailani Rose Faber is the name that I gave myself while I was in jail. It is a combination of my name and my children's names. I was trying to recreate myself and having a name that incorporated those that I loved the most helped me to feel closer to them, as well as to say what was really important to me. This was but a small part of my effort to reclaim my soul. The affirmation written above, and many others, was my way of claiming what I wanted for myself: peace, serenity and, most of all, hope for a new, better life.

The dragonfly, the lady bug, and the butterfly are all symbols of transformation and enlightenment. Looking back, it was as if I had been a ravenous caterpillar devouring all in its path that, at this point, had cocooned itself in a chrysalis that allowed it to rest, grow and transform into something beautiful. An integral part of that transformation was my spiritual quest to know the nature of God on an up-close and personal level.

Prisoners face a life situation that includes a unique set of circumstances that, preceded by crisis, compel them to aggressively

seek God. If you have never been in a jail or prison, but have been in an abusive relationship, you are in captivity as well. This is what happens:
- Your personal affairs are now in someone else's hands.
- Your ability to communicate with others is severely limited and controlled.
- Your emotions and state of mind are closely guarded and masked as a form of self-preservation.
- Your physical freedom has been taken away or severely limited.
- Affection, kindness and loving touches are withheld.
- You have little or no say about what your daily activities will be.
- You have been cut off from your loved ones.
- You feel powerless to fix or change your current situation.

This is where I suddenly found myself and why, without consciously doing so, I began diligently to seek God. Probably the most debilitating factor in the "hitting rock bottom" scenario described above is the last one—feeling powerless. It's also the one that tips the scales in God's favor. Whenever our egos are involved, it's very difficult to make a real connection with God. For someone like me, your overachieving control freak, it is impossible. And so my journey began.

On my first trip to the jail library (we were allowed to check out two books on each weekly visit) I picked out two mysteries from the fiction section hoping to escape my surroundings through the portal of my imagination. Over the next three weeks I struggled to read those books getting no further than fifty pages into either of them. I just couldn't get interested. My mind wandered and I finally gave up.

The next time I visited the library I found the spiritual section and picked out two books from there. One was on the history of the modern-day Pentecostal movement and the other was about spiritual growth. I devoured these two books and couldn't wait to get back to the library. For the first time since my incarceration, I began to feel a little bit of peace.

In addition to my new reading curriculum, I also began to try my hand at praying. That is not to say that I hadn't prayed up until that point. I started praying the moment the police officer told me that my fiancé was probably going to die and, if he did, I would be charged with felonious murder. This, mind you, was before the squad car ever left my house that night in June.

What is a prayer? "Please help me God" is a good one used often by people in crisis. It's not flowery or too wordy or vague. It's a succinctly affective prayer that gets the ball rolling. I started off with this simple prayer and eventually graduated to writing my own. Words have always been my friend, and as a creative person, it was a natural progression. This is one that gave me great comfort.

"Comfort Me"

Father Mother God, creator of all that is seen and unseen, divine force that runs in, through and all around me. Wrap your soft and gentle arms around my soul and fill me with your love and comfort. Shield me from all pain within the circle of your strong embrace. Rest my head a while against your ample breast. Hold me close and kiss my brow as I listen to the heartbeat of the universe pulsing softly within your chest. Rock me, oh so gently, in this place of warmth and peace. Hum softly a hymn of love until it resonates throughout my being. Yes, hold me, rock me, sooth me Lord. Calm my spirit and fill me with a knowing grace, a peace, an awakening. Awaken in me the memory of who I am. Remind me that I am not separate from you or my brothers and sisters whom you also cherish. It is only this knowledge, this knowing, that can banish all fear. Remind me that you and I are one Sweet Spirit. We are one in the loving arms of Christ Jesus, always and forever, amen.

In addition to this prayer, I started singing a prayer, over and over, on a regular basis. Songs can be prayers, too. Ever wonder why "Amazing Grace" is such a popular song? The lyrics are about receiving grace (God's assistance or strength) to get you through the really hard times. The song I sang was "Let There Be Peace On Earth." I sang this song over and over as I paced back and forth in my cell. I usually did this when I felt an anxiety attack coming on. I had several attacks during those first weeks. Come to find out, singing helps to stave off panic attacks by regulating your breathing. So, I got a double benefit, drawing closer to God while avoiding another stay in segregation. And, luckily, God doesn't care if you can carry a tune.

I also found comfort in reciting Unity's "Prayer for Protection." It goes like this:

The light of God surrounds me. The love of God enfolds me. The power of God protects me. The presence of God watches over me. Wherever I am, God is, and all is well.

I even wrote this out several times and gave copies to some of the women that I thought were hurting and open to receiving this kind of help. They all seemed grateful for either the gesture or the prayer itself.

In addition to my prayer life, I signed up for and attended every religious service available. It didn't matter if it was Catholic or Pentecostal. I was there praying my little heart out. I knew the Apostle's Creed by heart because I was raised Catholic. But I also prayed in tongues alongside the Pentecostals. I had dated a devout Christian at one point and he had taken me to a church where this was common. It came natural to me, if you can call this "natural." When I pray in tongues it sounds Asian. I can't explain it and can't begin to understand it, but it took me to a place that felt closer to God, and I liked that. I even went through a full-immersion baptism in the Greene County jail.

More important than my own prayers, I was putting Mark and my children on their prayer lists. They all had one and they promised that their congregations and prayer circles would pray for our loved ones daily. As Mark's condition improved and he moved from a 1% chance of living to 3% and 7% and 15% as each day passed, I came to believe with all my heart that the power of prayer was real and mighty. I understood on a deep level that when two or more come together in prayer, miracles happen. There must have been thousands of people praying for Mark because it didn't matter if I had put his name on their list before, I put it on there again and again, just for good measure.

In the evenings, several of the women would stand together in the middle of the pod and pray. We would hold hands, close our eyes and someone would lead us in prayer. We did it every night before we were banished to our cells at 11:00 pm. It was the closest thing to having a sense of family inside those walls that I would come to know during those five months.

And so my spiritual journey went—reading, praying and writing. I read the Bible from cover to cover. I borrowed one until the one I ordered came in. It seemed like forever. I loved that Bible. It had a handy book and chapter checklist in the back that I could check off as I read each one. I had read much of the Bible before, but never cover to cover. The Old Testament was difficult at times. I remember thinking that it was a miracle that there were any animals left on earth with all the goats, lambs and oxen that were slaughtered and burned as sacrifice to God. And the instructions on how far to defecate away from the fire, being sure to bury it when you're done, illustrated the ignorance of mankind. Not that there was not inspiration and beauty in the Old Testament. I loved Proverbs, Psalms and Ruth among others. But I got real nourishment from the New Testament.

My spiritual quest did not center completely on the Christian books and beliefs. I read the Koran and I read about the Buddha and I eventually returned to the path that is natural to me, the metaphysical. The last spiritual book, or book of any kind for that matter, that I read was Deepak Chopra's "The Seven Spiritual Laws." I finished it minutes before I walked out those cell doors for the last time. It was perfect. It wrapped up all of what I had learned in a beautiful package that felt like "truth" and I felt prepared to leave my cocoon.

COMFORTABLE WORDS

Words were very important to me during this time of tribulation. Words were a comfort and I tried very hard to create words that would comfort those that I loved. For me, the comfort came in the books I read, the sermons I listened to, the newspaper that my friend Wendy subscribed to for me, the prayers that I prayed, and the songs that I sang. As I reached out to my family and friends in letters, I also found solace, although unintentionally.

For my children, my first thought was to take their minds off of what had happened—to somehow lessen the impact and reduce the scars. The best way that I could think of to do this was to write them "Happy Memories" letters. In them, I described the good times that we had had together. I tried to recreate those moments in time when we were happy and content, with as much detail as possible. I shared with them my feelings of joy and my love for them at that particular moment.

My hope was that they would remember these times as well and think less about the night of the fire and our resulting separation. In doing so, I was able to escape my surroundings and circumstances and enjoy a brief reprise from my grief. When I ran out of happy memories to write about, I composed a "Future Happy Memory" letter in which I described a road trip to the beach with our dog, Mocha. It was the most detailed of all. I needed it to be detailed so that I could live every moment of it.

I tried to keep things light in order to allay their fears about where I was and how I was being treated. I had to lie a little about that. Some of the guards were nice and treated us like human beings, but most did not. I had never experienced such degradation in my life. But the kids didn't need to know that. I told them everyone was being very nice and taking good care of me.

In one letter I wrote about my schedule of activities, described my surroundings, my weekly menu, the Saturday movie night, and even some of the women who were there with me. I even drew a detailed floor plan of the "pod" which was returned to me as "unapproved" for delivery. I guess I could have been planning an escape, but the thought hadn't crossed my mind. That shows how little I knew about being a prisoner.

I'm sure some of my letters, if they read them, caused the corrections officers some concern about my sanity. Around Halloween, I wrote my son a letter about his alien father's planned visit to him. We used to joke that he was half human and half alien. After Michaela's father rejected him and his biological father made a less than enthusiastic effort to be in his life, we just made up a good story.

I wrote him one letter in Pig Latin. That was fun. I did word search and crossword puzzles and fill-in-the-blank letters for him to send back to me. He wasn't very good at writing letters, but what 10-year-old boys are? I made cards and drew pictures for them. I learned how to do "watercolors" with a rag, the comic section of the newspaper, and a stick of deodorant. Come to find out, they fade over time, but they smell good for a while and they are pretty while they last.

Some of my writing was dry, formal, filled with legal terminology and hand-produced in triplicate. I hadn't been in jail long when I was served with modification papers by my ex-husband. In it, he was requesting sole legal and physical custody of our daughter, limited supervised visitation for me, and, of course, child support.

I don't remember where I found the format or content for my response. I hadn't been to the library yet and I believe that the only thing I was requesting was to be at the hearing. In retrospect, showing up to the hearing in Greene County jail attire to plead my case would probably have done more harm than good. But my brain was still not fully functional and my emotions were all over the place. I couldn't have made a rational decision at that point, if my life depended on it.

I had my documents notarized and forwarded to the court then waited patiently for a response. None came. The day of the hearing came and my name was not on the call-out to be transported to the courtroom. I was devastated. And I was very angry. I felt like I had been victimized by my ex-husband, by the judge, and by the system. I had rights, didn't I? I followed protocol and submitted the required legal documents and I was ignored. I wasn't even worthy of a response.

I didn't like being a victim. In reality, I wasn't, but it was an easier title to hold than victimizer. It would be some time before that reality set in. Meanwhile, I had to pull myself out of the abyss of anger and blame and move up the emotional ladder to something more palatable. So I donned the robes of righteous indignation and turned my focus toward others who were victims…my fellow inmates.

Word got out that I could write, so I was soon approached by different women who needed my assistance. It seemed like it happened on a daily basis, but it may not have been that often. I just know that I filled out multiple applications for a public defender, wrote letters to judges and attorneys, and drew up several legal documents, once again in triplicate. Some of the women were illiterate, while others just couldn't find the right words, and none of them had the wherewithal to compose a legal motion. By helping them, I helped myself to feel less useless and definitely less worthless.

By far, the bulk of writing I did while incarcerated consisted of letters to Mark. During the five months I spent in Greene County Jail, I wrote him nearly a letter a day. In the beginning, I know that he was in a coma and was unable to read them. My sometimes fairytale, delusional thinking led me to fantasies of nurses and orderlies lovingly reading my letters to him as he lay there, somehow processing them in his subconscious, unconscious mind.

I had many different goals in writing my letters to him. They were to inform, to console, to entertain, to relate, and to prepare and warn. One of the first letters I wrote to him was one in which I advised him to run. I remember saying that if he wasn't arrested upon discharge from the hospital, that he needed to pack up and get as far away from Springfield, Missouri as possible.

At the time, I was scared—not only of my environment, but more importantly, of what my future held. With a $500,000 bond, 14 felonies and a possible murder charge looming, I was beginning to see many years in prison as a real possibility. I just knew that with Mark's criminal history, he was probably looking at even more years than I was. Mark was near the top of the Greene County Prosecutor's list of felons he most wanted to put away, so he would probably be facing even more charges. In fact, he wound up being charged with 17 felonies.

He didn't take my advice, thank goodness. In reality, I don't know that he ever read that letter. After my release and our reunification, much to my dismay, I learned that he had read very few of them. In his defense, he had a lot going on what with those daily burn debrasions, skin grafts, scar tissue removal, and physical therapy. Not to mention dealing with the emotional and psychological trauma of it all. So, reading my letters that he would probably have a hard time getting out of the envelope and holding in his hands was not high on his list of priorities.

When we were able to speak by telephone, he had to have someone answer the phone then lay it down on the bed. He then placed his palms on the side of the bed, did a half kneel and put his ear on it. His burns and bandages prevented him from holding the phone up to his face.

I'll never forget the first letter I got from him, because it came to me immediately after I sent him a very nasty one. I had just been placed in "the hole" for 30 days for possession of contraband and was feeling especially isolated and frustrated. Unfortunately, our letters crossed paths and I felt terrible when I got his funny, loving letter, complete with pictures. He drew two pictures of himself, front and back view, with shaded areas representing burned skin and un-shaded areas representing unburned skin.

Un-shaded areas included his feet, crotch, butt and head. How his head escaped scarring I can only attribute to an act of God because his entire head definitely got burned. In the picture he had a big smile on his face, as you can probably imagine, because his most valuable body parts had been spared.

He didn't write me often, but when he did, it was interesting. My letters to him were often very long, sometimes reaching 20 pages or more. Even though he may have never read them or received any kind of benefit from them, I know that I did. My letters were a journal of sorts that I was sharing with him. As in any journal, my writing allowed me to vent my frustrations and fears. They contained my hopes, dreams and aspirations, allowing me to turn my attention outside the jail walls and focus on a better future. My letters also helped me to lighten up by interjecting humor and creativity into my life and communication.

I remember one letter to Mark that was titled "How to Survive in Greene County Jail." It was a bullet point list of tips and tricks to make your life more comfortable. This included:

- Instructions on how to warm your cell by placing a wet piece of paper over your air vent
- How to alter a shampoo bottle to be used to create a stream of warm water rather than the cold, fine mist that normally comes from the shower head
- Alternate uses for jailhouse toothpaste including hanging pictures, scrubbing sinks, stain removal, etc.
- How to tweeze your eyebrows with two strings torn from the hem of your pants *(Not necessary for most men and some women.)*
- How to make an air freshener from a tube sock and baby powder that you swing in the air *(Very useful in a tiny cell with a cellie who has unlimited commissary funds and is gaining an average of five pounds per week.)*
- How to make your four inch flexi-pen rigid by wrapping a deodorant bottle sticker around it so you can use it without your hands cramping up

There were more, but I can't remember them all. I've been thinking lately of contacting Mark to ask for the letters, or copies of them. My problem is that I haven't spoken to him in years. He has moved on and a sudden, out-of-the blue call congratulating him on his new marriage with a closing request for copies of the letters may come off as insincere and self-serving. Honestly, it would be.

It's not that I don't care about him and his happiness. I have been thinking about contacting him for the past couple of years, but I never found the nerve. I also didn't want to "open that can of worms" as they say. I would really like to collect all of the letters I wrote over the five months that I was in jail. I would have my second book right there and it would be an experience to read the progression of my growth from the first to the last day.

My daughter kept all of my letters and cards in a shoe box. She brought them with her to one of our family counseling sessions. We used them in therapy to work through some of the things I said and she shared the thoughts and feelings that she had about them. She misplaced the box briefly and was very upset about it, but later found it.

I was able to gather many of the letters that I wrote to my son as he had kept them, or at least some of them. I also have letters that my mother kept and gave to me. My sister kept some that I wrote to my nephew and she sent me copies. I have some of the letters that I wrote to my sister, some of them nice and some not so nice. She sent me the copy of "Unspoken Promises" that begins this book and she remembered a children's book that I wrote called "Angel Kisses" that I had sent to her asking her to find an illustrator. I had even forgotten that I wrote that one. At this writing, she is still looking for it.

As I said in the prologue, I have always identified myself as a writer and dreamed of being published some day. I'm in my fifties now and, having lived a life filled with many mistakes, I sometimes curse my longing to be wise. It took me decades to figure out that the only way to become wise is either to sit at the feet of wise men and listen carefully to their words, or to make many, many mistakes and learn from them. Unfortunately, I chose the latter, more difficult path.

I now seek wisdom from other more advanced souls and try to emulate them. This is my spiritual quest. Part of turning a negative into a positive is passing this wisdom and, more importantly, hope onto others who may wish to get off the difficult path. That is the goal of my writing today, much as it was then—to give comfort to others.

LOVE AND LOSS

It wasn't until much later in my life that I realized that all men were not like my father. Not all men could meet a woman with three young children, marry her and raise her children as if they were his own. I know that he loved us as he did his two sons from his first marriage because, not long after he married my mom, he adopted all three of us. Even before that, he was our dad. We had no concept of "biological" versus "adopted" in our family, anymore than we recognized each other as "half" brothers or sisters. We were a family.

I had been out of treatment for about one month on the day my father died. My mother, father, Mark, my son and I were paying a visit to my great aunt and uncle who lived in Clinton, Missouri. It was New Year's Eve in 2004. The ride there was unremarkable. We all rode in the van and talked about whatever families talk about during the holidays, but when we arrived at my aunt and uncle's trailer everything changed.

Mark, Logan and I all hopped out of the van and headed inside. Mark and I went in to say hello to my Aunt Glondale and Uncle Raymond. My uncle was very ill and in a hospital bed in the living room. I introduced Mark to them both, kissed Uncle Raymond and looked out the screen door. My son was standing behind my mom and dad as she tried to help him up the three steps of the front porch.

My father was a double-amputee due to his diabetes and was going very slowly. I think he had a cane, possibly two canes. As I watched, he stopped on the first step to rest while my mother supported him by his arm. After a few seconds, he attempted the second step and then the third. He immediately sat down on a bench and said he couldn't breathe. I believe it was Aunt Glondale who suggested that I run an oxygen line out to him from the system that was installed in their trailer for my uncle.

It seemed like it took forever to find the oxygen tube and pull it out to the porch, but I was a bit panicked. I finally gave it to my mother and she placed it around his head and put the tube in his nose. Less than a minute later, he fell forward and collapsed onto the porch. I immediately rolled him onto his back, yelled for someone to call 911, and began CPR.

I had never done CPR in a real emergency situation. I was trained in it when I worked as a lifeguard many years before, but this was real. It was too real. My family watched as I gave chest compressions and breathed into his mouth. I think I knew immediately that it was useless when I heard his wet, bubbly exhalations. It was obvious even to me that his lungs were full of fluid. No amount of CPR could change the fact that he was in congestive heart failure and the oxygen could not get past all the water in his lungs.

It took about five minutes for the ambulance to arrive and the EMT's took over. I remember watching them and thinking that they were doing CPR wrong, pressing on his stomach, not his chest. It made me want to scream. After a few minutes of this with no pulse, they pronounced him deceased, and covered him up. The EMT's took some information from my mother and told her what funeral home he would be taken to. We were all in shock. What was supposed to be a pleasant outing to pay a holiday visit to family turned out to be one of the saddest days of our lives.

The ride home was quiet except for the occasional sound of sobbing. I was driving, but don't really remember the trip home. We were listening to some country station as we neared Cassville when Ray Price came on singing "For the Good Times." It reminded me of my dad and how he used to like to slow dance to his favorite old-time country songs. I realized I would never dance with my father again, or be forced to listen to Christmas carols in August, or hear him tell me blonde jokes, or any other number of things only he did. That's when I knew he was really gone.

When my little brother died it was no less painful and much more shocking. He was only 41 and seemingly healthy. In fact, he was a beast. He worked out religiously and was probably a little too obsessed with his body. As a Missouri Highway Patrolman, his life was in danger a lot, so he tried to make himself as big and scary as possible. I think it was his way of trying to make his wife less frightened by his chosen profession.

He took supplements that may have included steroids which could partially explain his sudden demise. Another reason was that he lost the genetic lottery with his biological father's inherited health issues. Whatever the reasons were, it didn't make it any easier to handle. What made it worse was that I believe he was still mad at me on the day he died.

We were never really close after he left the Marine Corp. The Corp changed him. In his youth he was a friendly, jovial, fun-loving guy. When he got out, he was serious, stern, and not much fun at all—at least not in my experience of him. The years he did in Iraq as a reservist only solidified this persona. I don't know if he saw any action there, but my sweet little brother was gone forever.

On June 12, 2007, my brother was at his father-in-law's home doing something with his horses. He had been having chest pains that he described as an intense heartburn feeling. The doctors did an endoscopic procedure and didn't find anything. He was scheduled for a stress test, but never made it to that appointment. While at his father-in-law's house, the pain became worse so he drove himself to the hospital. At some time during the examination his heart stopped beating. I think they were able to bring him back once or twice, but then he was dead. A relatively young man with three children, one only three years old, was dead.

In addition to the obvious pain of losing my little brother, what made it worse was that I would never be able to finally tear down that wall that stood between us for the past three years. All of the pain and resentment was left just floating there, never to be resolved. I like to imagine that my brother exists on the other side as the worry-free, happy kid that he used to be. Free of the world's pressures to be something more, something better, perhaps he is happy and, on some level, aware that I have made great changes in my life. Perhaps he has finally forgiven me.

When I told my father that I was going to stay in the relationship with Mark, he said, "Well, if you love him, there must be something good in him." As much as he wanted to blame Mark for everything that had happened, my dad realized that I was a grown woman who had made a series of bad decisions. Nobody held a gun to my head and Mark was not the problem. I was.

Throughout our marriage, I continued to make mistakes, but Mark held firm to his resolve to change his life. It appeared to me that he was having an easier time of it than I was. And maybe he was. Maybe it was because he had been through really hard times earlier in his life. His childhood was less than ideal and you could say he had gone through the school of hard knocks.

But that isn't why I believe he has done so well since the fire. I believe that it is because he possesses a spirit that is filled with optimism. He has the innate ability to see the bright side of everything. He is patient, loving and kind. Everyone who knows him knows that they could call him at any time, for any need, and he would be there with a smile and an open heart, willing to lend a hand.

Mark contributed to my recovery in so many ways, probably the best being his infectious positive attitude. It helped me to overcome my morose, depressive existence and become the outgoing, "glass half full" person that I am today. His patience and tolerance of my negative attitudes and negative behaviors supported me when I needed it the most. Most of all, he was my best friend.

Losing him, our friendship, and our love, was one of the most difficult parts of my story. Our marriage ended not because of our relationship, but because of our relationships with our children. I came to a place where I felt like I had to choose, and I chose my kids. I believe it was the right decision, but that doesn't make it any easier, although I would do it again. Even though we have both moved on in our lives, I still miss my best friend.

Life is full of pain and loss and the Universe doesn't care if this is a good time or not. One month out of treatment was not a good time for my father to die, but when would be a good time? It wasn't a good time for a 41-year-old man, with young children to die, either. Would later have been any less painful for the people who loved him? I can't answer that question.

I've met many men who have lost mothers, fathers, brothers, sisters, grandparents, cousins and friends while they were locked up and unable to grieve with their loved ones. In that respect, I guess I was lucky. I had Mark in my life when I needed him most, so I guess I was lucky there too. The point is, pain happens, and we can't use it as an excuse to fall apart. In fact, when our loved ones are watching us from the other side is the time to be the strongest. That is the time to be the people they will be proud of. That is what will help them to truly rest in peace.

SUPERNATURAL

I couldn't tell my story without telling the story of the spirits and angels that worked so hard to save me from myself and my addiction. Have you ever noticed how certain places have an aura or feeling that hits you as you walk in the door? I can remember the exact day that the aura of my home changed. Initially, it felt light, open and inviting. And then, overnight, it didn't.

Mark and I had been up all night after he moved in. He had a coffee table that was a jaguar base with a glass top. I spent most of the evening spray painting it a glossy black while Mark was busy doing something that tweakers do. The jaguar was looking beautiful at one point, but as meth addicts are wont to do, I couldn't leave it alone. I put too many coats on and put it outside, in the humid air to dry. Then I fell asleep.

When I woke up, the jaguar was no longer a glossy black, the feeling in my house was now dark, and the atmosphere was thick with a sense of foreboding. This was the first sign of a shift in the spiritual energy. One might even say a spiritual war had begun to be waged. On one side was this dark force that wielded its influence in and through me and my addiction. On the other, spirits who cared for me while they were alive watched over me and were trying to warn me off the path that I was on.

Not everyone knows this but when there is a strong spiritual presence around, electrical anomalies occur. In my house it was the lighting in the basement which happened to be where we did most of our "cooking" and using. The light at the bottom of the stairs was particularly vexatious. I must have changed that bulb every few months. The most costly, however, were the flood lamps inset in the ceiling throughout the recreation room. I kept replacing the constantly burning out bulbs with 10-year bulbs, yet they each lasted no more than four or five months.

My daughter has a friend who lives in that neighborhood right now. When she told her friend where she used to live, the friend told her that everyone in the neighborhood believes that the house is haunted. She may be right. There were a few times when some strange things happened—things that could not be explained by a shared delusion or hallucination of two meth heads.

On one occasion, Mark and I were sitting downstairs in the office doing something, I don't remember what, when we heard what sounded like children running across the floor above our heads. We immediately thought our kids were home, but they were supposed to be at school, so we were puzzled and a little alarmed. We jumped up and ran upstairs to see what was going on. There was no one there.

Another time I was in my bathroom putting on makeup when I heard the children's bathroom cabinet slam shut. I was alone in the house so I went to investigate. I played with the door seeing if it would stay open thinking it had been left open and just shut on its own. It was on a hinge though so it was either open or closed, no in between. That could not have happened and it didn't make sense. I thought about it for a minute then quickly finished putting on my makeup and left the house.

What I really want to share with you is the story of the angels who were there watching over me and my family in the weeks and months before the fire. The first "save" occurred for my step-daughter, Ali. It was not the most spectacular save, but it was amazing nonetheless.

The stories in this chapter may sound like hallucinations or delusional by-products of a drug-addled mind. That is why I haven't spoken about these events much or even shared it with anyone who wasn't there. One person who was there during this time, and who was not under the influence, is my son Logan who was 10 at the time.

I spoke with him about this recently and he recounted his version of the event as he saw it unfold. As it turns out, our versions match on all of the important details, although I had mistakenly thought that he had been riding bikes with his step-sister when he was not.

Evidently, my son was the one who created the scenario for this miracle to occur. From my perspective standing in the driveway, I didn't see him come out of the kitchen door leading into the garage. Ali was riding her bicycle very fast down the street in front of the house. I believe she had asked me and Mark to watch her and that is why we were both witnesses.

When Logan came out of the door, our dog Mocha ran past him and made a beeline straight for the street. What I saw was Ali speeding down the street and Mocha coming out of nowhere, running behind a parked car and converging in terrifying slow motion with the front tire of her bike.

The next scene was straight out of the movie "Angels in the Outfield." As Mocha ran directly in front of Ali, she hit the dog and then flew directly over her handle bars through the air coming down slowly toward the pavement. We all watched in horror envisioning what would surely end in a trip to the emergency room.

But instead of bouncing off the street as would be expected, she seemed to float just inches above it. Due to the forward momentum of her fall, her body flew this way somewhere between 15 and 20 feet down the street. Both Logan and I agreed on this estimate. When she finally stopped, she stood up and ran over to me and her dad.

I was in shock. I remember cursing and crying hysterically because I had just witnessed what I was sure should have included horrible cuts, scrapes and possibly broken bones. I was shaking all over. Mark, much calmer, checked Ali over from head to toe and found only a small scratch on her right wrist and a very small strawberry on her hip. She was fine.

To this day, Mark says that his mother, for whom Ali was named, was the one who kept her aloft and landed her gently on the street. The next year, I had a similar experience, except my guardian angel literally saved my life.

This incident requires some background information in order to explain how I got myself into this precarious situation. Mark had a friend, or using buddy rather, who was living in the house that Mark lived in before he moved in with me. It was in an older building that probably used to be a garage that was converted into a small home.

To get into the house, you had to climb a set of stairs that led to a porch on the second floor where the front door was. A bedroom was in the lower level while the kitchen, living room and bathroom were upstairs. There was a paved drive that led up to the house. On the left was a duplex and on the right the drive changed to gravel and dropped off sharply into a large vacant lot next to an abandoned commercial building. It was not in the best part of town.

The friend, Rick (not his real name), was using meth pretty heavily and was having some serious psychotic side-effects. He was extremely paranoid and having delusions and hallucinations. It was becoming very annoying to have him calling and coming over constantly to tell us what he thought was happening and what he was seeing. He described ninjas with McDonald's bags over their heads trying to get into the house. This was the funniest, but not the weirdest.

At one point, Mark and I sat outside the house in the early morning hours after promising Rick that we would catch them in the act. It was a long boring night. Next, we installed video cameras and a VCR so that he could record it and show us these malicious intruders as they were harassing him.

On the night of my biggest miracle, Rick had called us to come over and watch a video in which he claimed he had proof of someone climbing up his front porch in the middle of the night. We were dubious, but went over nonetheless, at least to humor him. As we watched his video evidence it became clear that he was seriously disturbed.

He showed us video that had absolutely nothing on it except a dark empty porch. When we said we didn't see anything, he became incensed. He pointed to the screen asking us why we couldn't see the hands on the rails. He showed us what he said was the thumb and the fingers. If these were an intruder's hands, he would have had to be ten feet tall with hands bigger than Tony Robbins', but he wouldn't listen to reason.

The only thing to do was prove it to him, so I had this brilliant idea to climb outside the railing and place my hands where he was pointing in the video so that he could see that it just wasn't possible. So we all went outside and I climbed over the rail on the corner farthest away from the stairs. I was fine until I grasped a large wooden ball on the top of the corner post for support in preparation to climb around to the front. As I did so, the ball came loose from the railing and my hands went straight up in the air with it. I began to fall straight back toward the ground.

The ground I was falling toward was the sloping gravel to the right of the driveway, about twelve to fifteen feet down. I forgot to mention that there was a large piece of rebar that stuck straight up out of the ground in that very spot. I remember falling back, the wooden ball still in my hands, looking up at the stars thinking I am about to be impaled on that spike—that my life was over.

The next thing I knew, I was landing on my feet, on the opposite side of the driveway, about eight feet from the bottom of the steps as I shouted "I'm okay!" Mark said he also thought I would surely have been impaled on that rebar as he screamed my name and looked over the railing, expecting to see my bloody body directly below him. When I shouted "I'm okay," he turned and saw me standing on the opposite corner of the house. He couldn't believe it, and neither could I.

Not even a cat could pull off that kind of contortionist move by flying sideways across that much space and landing in an upright position. To this day, I'm sure there was angelic intervention that saved me from my own stupidity. I believe that my guardian angel knew that there were bigger plans for my life that required my survival.

There were many angels and spirits of loved ones who intervened, or tried to, during those days, but Edie was the first one to show her face. Edie was a friend of mine. Actually, she was more like a grandmother to me. I'm not sure why, but I felt very close to her in life, and even in death. She owned a daycare for newborn to two-year-olds that she ran from her home. Both my children stayed with her while I worked. She was extremely down to earth and just what you would call "good people."

I did some free-lance work for her—a newsletter and various applications for funding for her daycare. We also socialized, went camping with our families, and I would often just stop by to chat. When she passed away from a sudden heart attack, I felt like I had lost part of my family. Her kids asked me to write her obituary which I was happy to do. At her funeral, as I stood up in the pews during a final prayer, I felt her hand touch my shoulder. It sent shivers up my spine, but I wasn't scared. I knew it was just her telling me she wasn't really gone. As they wheeled her casket out of the church, the alarms went off. People laughed, and said, "That's Edie. Making a grand exit."

Flash forward to the night of the fire. I was coming home from running errands. As I pulled my van into the garage, I hit the automatic garage door opener to close the door behind me. As I always did, I looked in my rear view mirror to make sure it was going down and wouldn't hit the bumper. This time when I looked in the mirror, I saw Edie's face, peering at me from the back row seats. It startled me, but I wasn't frightened. She was only there for a few seconds and then disappeared. My first thought was that she had come to warn me. I even told Mark that I saw Edie and something bad was going to happen. I wish I had had the presence of mind to heed the warning.

My father, on the other hand, has visited me several times since his passing. His visits did not start until Christmas of 2010. That was the year that my daughter was reunited with us. My dad loved Christmas more than anything. He would start playing Christmas carols right after Labor Day. Honestly, sometimes he wouldn't wait that long. But putting up the tree was his favorite part of the holiday. Well, he didn't put up the tree. He supervised while the kids did it. That was the one day of the year that he would pour himself a Crown Royal, sit in his chair and drink it as he directed us in where to hang bulbs and how much tinsel to put on the tree. Some years you couldn't see the lights through all the tinsel. He loved tinsel.

It was December of 2010 and Michaela and I were putting up our tree in the house in Monett. I had purchased it a few years back from a thrift store for $2.00. It was pre-lit, except when I got it home only two of the four strands of lights worked. Eventually, only one strand worked, but I just added more lights. After all, it only cost me $2.00.

On this night, we were listening to Christmas music on the satellite and unpacking ornaments from boxes. I had already put the tree together and plugged it in. Of course, the one strand of lights is all that lit up. Michaela was watching me from the couch and we were talking when "The Little Drummer Boy" came on. My breath caught in my throat and I looked at her saying "This was Papa's favorite Christmas song." Then I started to cry. I missed him terribly.

Just then, Michaela's eyes got really big and she pointed over my shoulder at the tree. "Look momma," she said. I turned around and saw that all four strands of lights on the tree were lit. I smiled and then I knew it was my dad. I knew in my heart that he was there to say "Merry Christmas. I see how well you're doing, and I'm proud of you."

Since then, he has come to say "Happy Birthday," "Happy Thanksgiving," and "Merry Christmas" on more than one occasion. Sometimes only Harlie, my dog, sees him. She will stand up, along with the hair on her back, and start to growl at something unseen. Usually though, he does something with electricity, messing with the lights, or the music—playing our favorite dance song when we were little which was "Sugar Sugar" by the Archies—usually when I'm thinking about him. This Christmas he changed the channel on my television, twice just in case I wasn't absolutely sure it was him. "Merry Christmas, Dad. I love you, too," I told him. It's comforting to know that he sees how far I've come, but even more, to know that this is not all there is.

WRESTLING WITH MY DEMONS

Before I got to a place where I could be proud of myself and know that my loved ones were proud of me, too, I wrestled with my demons. I felt tremendous guilt and shame about what I had done. It wasn't so much about what I had done, but that I had brought my children along for the ride. If I am to be perfectly honest, this is something that I continue to struggle with.

In the early days after the fire, the guilt was bad, but the shame was extreme. Shame is a terrible thing. As I learned later, guilt is feeling bad about something you've done, but shame is feeling bad about who you are. Or, in other words, it's "I DID something bad" versus "I AM something bad." I definitely felt like I was a bad mother, if not a bad person, and being a good mother is what I had always wanted and tried to be. This was a colossal failure on my motherhood report card.

I was blessed enough to receive custody of my son when I finished my 28-day, inpatient treatment. My mother had a temporary custody arrangement with the Division of Family Services. When I was released from treatment, I went to live at my parents' house in Cassville. My mom just got a job in Oregon where she could actually use her doctorate in a position at a community college there, so she was preparing to move. DFS made a follow-up call, spoke with my mom, and never contacted me again.

My daughter was a different story. Her father had filed for sole legal and physical custody of her while I was in jail. I filed papers myself soon after and tried to be present at the hearing, but I was never allowed to do so. What followed were painful years of supervised visitation and awkward nightly phone calls.

It was 2009 before I felt worthy of trying to get "normal" visitation privileges and 2010 before it came to fruition. The intervening years were the most difficult of my life. Having her father accompany us on all of our visits, seemingly judgmental and condemning, was excruciating as he watched us in the background. There were verbal altercations when I got behind on my child support. And once, he smelled alcohol on my breath and confronted me.

Alcohol had become my new addiction. I used to tell myself a story about my drinking that placed a lot of blame on my nurse practitioner for taking me off of my psychotropic medications too quickly. I went into withdrawal from Geodon when she cut me off cold turkey and I turned to alcohol to stop the shakes, racing heart and sweats. I have Bipolar II Disorder and was on three different meds when I was released from treatment. In 2006, I could no longer receive my medications for free, so I stopped driving to Joplin to get them.

Even as I sit here writing this chapter I realize that I was abusing alcohol long before this happened. It just got really bad after I was taken off the Geodon. I used to come home from work and immediately pour myself a drink—either whiskey and Coke, or vodka and Sprite. I wasn't hiding it then, even when my son came home and found me passed out on the living room floor one evening. Mark described me as a "zombie" that just sat on the couch, drinking, smoking and staring blankly at the television. I wouldn't even respond when spoken to.

There were more embarrassing instances that resulted from my constant states of intoxication that I won't go into. What came of it was my husband calling my probation officer and telling him that I was drinking. This was after several fights in which I promised to stop and he became increasingly frustrated with me. What he didn't know is that I was numbing myself to the overwhelming sense of shame and feelings of failure that I just couldn't endure. Being sober meant having to look at myself in the mirror, under stark lights, that revealed my flaws in all of their ugly detail. These were the character defects that I wasn't ready to face.

The alcohol abuse was just a symptom of the problem and the problem was shame. I saw myself as a failure, a loser, a terrible mother, and a fraud. Everything that I had prided myself on was gone. The good mother, the entrepreneur, the home-owner, no longer described me. I had lost everything and had no one to blame but myself. Not that I didn't try.

I harbored a lot of anger at my ex-husband because I knew that he was the one who first called the police to alert them to our illegal activities. I was angry at my sister for selling all my possessions and paying me only a fraction of what they were worth. And the ironic part is that I was angry at my brother for his judgmental inability to forgive me and give me the benefit of the doubt. It was ironic because this is the same thing that I was doing to myself.

Exacerbating this entire mess was my Bipolar Disorder. This is a diagnosis that I was first given when I was nineteen. I was given the same diagnosis again in my thirties, and for the final time when I entered drug treatment at Lafayette House. Each time I dismissed the diagnosis, refused to take the medication, or quit taking it soon after I started. Everything that I had read about it just didn't sound like me.

The third time I was diagnosed, the doctors put me on the usual three-pronged approach with an antidepressant, antipsychotic and anticonvulsant. This cocktail is supposed to keep you stable. What it did was keep me depressed and, thanks to the antipsychotic, I was also feeling very drugged. Changes in my dosages didn't seem to help and my communication with my nurse practitioner probably wasn't what it should have been. Take this scenario and pour alcohol on top of it and you get a really messed up individual.

It wasn't until I started my graduate degree in clinical psychology and learned that there are two types of Bipolar Disorder that I realized that the doctors were right. I just wish that they had told me what type I had and had described the symptoms for me. People with Bipolar II don't have the extremely high manic episodes that Type I's have. They are hypomanic, meaning the highs are not as high. It looks a lot like someone who is tweaking. It includes what is called "pressured speech," an inability to sleep, extreme creativity and high levels of productivity.

The lows, or depressive episodes, look a lot like someone coming down off of meth. You just want to sleep all the time, you have no energy, and functioning is minimal. There is a high frequency of people with Bipolar Disorder who also abuse meth. Some doctors even diagnose meth addicts with Bipolar almost automatically. I'm not sure if they know about this correlation or they just don't know enough to allow the person to get some clean time and return to normal before they make sweeping judgments about a person's mental health. Mark was even diagnosed as Bipolar when he was in the nursing home and he is about as far from Bipolar as you can get.

Because I was diagnosed long before I ever used stimulants, I could at least take this possibility out of the equation. As I learned about the symptoms and matched them with my behaviors over my lifetime, I was able to come to terms with it. I know that I cannot take an antidepressant alone, or at least not in a very high dose, because it sends me into a hypomanic state. I also know that I have to get adequate sleep or the same thing will happen. Finals weeks were always interesting for my family as I usually got very little sleep and they would have to tell me to go to bed or stay in the other room because I was getting on their nerves.

But before I could deal with my Bipolar Disorder, I had to deal with my alcohol abuse. I stopped one time in the fall of 2006, but the ice storm of 2007 seemed like a good reason to buy some beer and it went downhill from there. I went to Alcoholics Anonymous for those few months and thought I was doing well. I was not utilizing my sponsor though and everyone in recovery knows a good sponsor will make all the difference.

When I relapsed in 2007, I began to sneak the alcohol. I had it hidden in a low cupboard, behind the appliances that we never use, or the Tupperware that completely filled one cabinet. I even brought it to school in my back pack that first semester at Missouri State. On the way home from school I would stop at a convenience store and buy a half-pint of vodka to drink on the way home if I was out. But I wasn't fooling anybody. Mark could smell it on my breath and there were nights when I would pass out or wake up and wander around the house looking for the bathroom.

It all came to a head on May 21, 2007. Logan was the only one home and I was fixing a roast and mashed potatoes for dinner. I decided to run to the store to pick up a gallon of vodka because I was out. I chugged quite a bit on the way home which was only one mile. Chugging it straight from the bottle was my new way of drinking.

I don't remember much after that. When I woke up the next day my hand hurt and nobody in the family was speaking to me. In the kitchen I found a bowl of mashed potatoes on the top shelf of the refrigerator and the pork roast was sitting in the crock pot shredded up with the string that holds it together mixed into it. There was salsa on the floor in front of the refrigerator and spilled inside.

I found out later that I had made the potatoes and nobody could find them. I then used the mixer on the roast. Why I would do that is unclear but I'm sure my vodka soaked brain thought it made perfect sense. I guess I also spilled the salsa out of the refrigerator, probably when I was putting the potatoes away.

My hand hurt because I had fallen and tried to catch myself on the sofa table. My hand was broken, but I don't know if the table fell on my hand or I just broke it trying to break my fall. That was the last time that I drank alcohol.

I returned to the tables of A.A., got a good sponsor, and started working the steps in earnest. As I started to repair my relationship with my family, and myself, I also began to feel human again. My mood lifted and I started to function normally. I still took medications, but they worked much better and I was eventually able to stop using anything altogether. May 22, 2007 is my clean date from all mind-altering substances. It is also the day I started to really live. It is when the real healing began.

RESENTMENTS AND REGRETS

I believe that the largest contributing factor to my ongoing struggle with alcohol was my anger. I wasn't discriminatory about who I directed that anger toward. You could also call it blame and resentment. I resented everyone whom I believed played a part in my ever using meth, helping me to stop using meth, punishing me for using meth, judging me for using meth, and taking advantage of me while I was using meth.

The list is so long. It includes Mark, my sister, my ex-husband, my mother, the prosecutors, the judge, my brother, my fellow tweakers and meth cooks, and, of course the detectives and other law enforcement. This anger burned inside of me like a torch and although, like all fire, it caused pain, I continued to hang onto it. I don't think I even realized at the time that it was there. At least I didn't consciously recognize what I was doing or what it was doing to me.

I love the saying "Hanging onto resentments is like taking poison and expecting the other person to die." All the while, the other person is living their life, oblivious, and probably quite happy, not giving you a second thought. It's ridiculous when you think about it. Yet we addicts do it anyway feeling self-righteous and indignant in our delusional perception of injury and victimization.

But it serves a greater purpose and that's because blaming others feels more comfortable in our bodies and our psyche's than taking responsibility for our own actions. Actions begin with choices. To acknowledge and accept that we are 100% responsible for the devastation of our own lives and victimization, not only of ourselves, but of everyone who loves us and whom we love, requires a huge shift in consciousness. It's a painful shift, but one worth taking.

I don't know when this shift occurred in me, but it eventually did. I'd love to say that this is when things began to improve, but that would be a lie. Things got worse before they got better. It's kind of like lancing a boil. It's scary, very painful and a little disgusting to look at, but it has to be done before you can begin to heal. It takes a lot of self-reflection that often initially takes you to a place of guilt and shame.

This feels even worse than resentment. That's why so many of us refuse to go there. For me, a lot of this shame centered around the fact that, as a woman and a mother, I did not have custody of my young daughter. The pain was made worse every time I saw a mother with her daughter. I remember seeing a mom with her young daughter coming out of Wal-Mart one time. They were holding hands and laughing. It brought me to tears.

The worst times were when I would be talking about my daughter with someone and, although I tried very hard to hide it, the fact that she did not live with me would come out. I could see the judgment on their faces and my own face would turn red with embarrassment and shame. Children always go with the mother in divorce, don't they? If they don't, then the mother must be a really horrible person who did something despicable. That's what I thought and what I was sure they were thinking. And the shame consumed me.

And oh the regrets! Shoulda, woulda, coulda filled my thoughts for countless moments of the day. In my imagination I rewrote history over and over lingering there in what might have been my happy life enjoying the laughter and smiles of happiness on my children's faces; continuing as a successful business owner; respected by my peers and the rest of society. Being able to look in the mirror and see a self-confident, self-respecting woman. If only I had done things differently.

At first my regrets focused on the night of the fire. Why didn't we just leave the meth lab in the hidden closet? They would never have found it. Or why didn't I just take Mark to the hospital myself after I put the fire out? All ridiculous thoughts! Neither one would have stopped us from being arrested and, face it, I needed to be. We both needed to be arrested. Something had to happen to stop the madness.

When enough time passed, my regrets focused on Mark. Why did I ever get involved with him? If only I had told John "no" when he asked me to get some cocaine. I would never have called Mark, wound up with meth instead of cocaine, and begun my relationship with him and that evil drug. But then I would turn my attention to John. Why did I listen to him when he asked me to get drugs? I hadn't done drugs in several years. I had put that behind me. I should have told him "no."

After it started, I could have put a stop to it at several junctures. The first time we were raided would have been a good time. That should have been my wake-up call. Who sees their children go through that kind of trauma—guns pointed at them, doors breaking open as they hang up their coats, seeing their mom hauled off in handcuffs—and decides to continue down the same destructive path? Certainly not someone whose brain has been hijacked by drugs.

I don't know exactly how long the resentments and regrets lingered. It was years, but I'm not sure how many. During this time, my emotional wounds festered. They eventually became scars, but not the scars of a warrior. They were scars of a victim. I would try to hide them, but that was impossible. Anyone who looked at me knew I was wounded by the way I carried myself, communicated with others, and presented myself to society.

I cut my hair short, quit wearing make-up and took no pride in my appearance. Maybe I subconsciously wanted my outside to match what I believed about myself on the inside. I was ugly. My soul was ugly and unlovable. If someone complimented me, I would brush it off telling myself, "If they only knew."

At this point my resentments turned inward and I began to loathe myself and who I had become. This was about the same time that I began abusing alcohol. In a way, it was a step in the right direction. I had begun to take responsibility for my circumstances, but it is a much more painful emotional state—guilt and shame—than blame is. It's also more destructive to the psyche, yet it is where you have to start in order to start to turn things around. You just can't hang out there.

I can't pinpoint a moment in time, or an epiphany, when things began to turn around. I can't even say with certainty that I am 100% healed of this emotional poisoning. I am definitely over the resentments, but sometimes I still struggle with regrets, although I believe that I am almost there.

As time goes on, I see the gift in all of this. I will never stop regretting causing pain for my children, but I now see the good that has and will continue to come out of my past mistakes. Who I have become and what I can now contribute to changing society and future generations is becoming more and more evident to me.

I've learned that I am not a victim of circumstance. Every experience I have had, I have drawn to me. Every difficult person who has harmed me has been a great teacher. Although I don't consider myself wise, I am definitely smarter and less naïve than I was in my youth. If I had not gone through everything that I have, I would not be the happy and successful person that I am today. By successful, I mean living an abundant life filled with positive emotions and relationships, meaning and achievement.

You've probably heard the saying, "The best revenge is a life well-lived." To me, that means proving all the naysayers wrong by becoming someone that others look up to, rather than down on. It means embracing those who criticized, judged, and pushed me away by forgiving them. It means coming to an understanding that people judge what they cannot comprehend and often fear. And also, realizing that they often are repulsed by the things they don't want to recognize in themselves. It's that other famous quote in action—"There, but for the grace of God, go I."

THERE'S NO PLACE LIKE HOME

What is a home? What is homeless? For me, a home is a place to call your own. A safe place to keep your stuff, a place to make good memories with your family, a place where you can go that makes you feel like a normal person. Homeless is not having this in your life.

I wasn't homeless in that I lived on the street, but for almost a year, my family lived in conditions that were temporary and unsecure. After my father passed, my mother stayed in Oregon and used the insurance money from his death to finish remodeling their home in Cassville. This is where I was staying with Mark and my son.

My brother was overseeing the renovations as he was going to purchase the house when it was complete. My mom wouldn't allow him to kick us out so we lived there during the remodeling and adding on phase. We migrated to the back bedroom, hung plastic sheets up to keep the sheetrock dust out, and tried to stay out of the way.

Mark and I helped out with the construction where we could to try to earn our keep. We tore out walls, ripped up floor tiles, sanded concrete, and even plumbed the bathrooms. At times, we had no bathroom facilities and eventually no kitchen. We had heat in the winter, but when the warm months came, there was no air conditioning, so we placed a window fan in the bedroom and tried to stay cool.

Throughout this time, the tension between me and my brother's family became palpable. Mark's daughter had a cat that her mother did not want, so it came to live with us. This became a bone of contention between us. They didn't want a cat in their house which is understandable. I think it was messing upstairs which upset my sister-in-law. Eventually, they complained to my mother enough that she said we had to go.

We moved to a motel across from the golf course on Highway 112. It consisted of a little cabin that had a kitchenette, bathroom and a bedroom. Mark and I stayed in the living room that had a pull-out sofa bed while the kids stayed in the bedroom. And of course, Mocha and the cat were there too.

If it wasn't for my mom, we would have been homeless, because she generously paid our weekly rent. By this time Mark's disability had been approved and he was getting a monthly check that helped us pay for food, gas and other necessities. I had an acquaintance from Lafayette House who hooked me up with a job cleaning condominiums in Branson.

I drove down a few times a week in our Geo Metro that Mark paid $200 for before the fire. It wasn't exactly reliable, but it got good gas mileage and it worked, until it didn't. We also had our 1996 Dodge Caravan that Mark signed over to mom after the fire. She signed it back over to us when I got out of jail.

I made a deal with the owners of the motel to clean rooms between customers and they took some money off our weekly fees. It was the only way I could feel like I was contributing to our keep. I hated that at 42 years-old, my family was being taken care of by my mother. She was the only reason we had a roof over our heads. When I told her I would pay her back, she would say "You can take care of me when I'm old." We're only 17 years apart in age and I always said we'd be sitting on the front porch of the old folks' home rocking in our chairs together. I know that her retirement fund would be much fatter if it weren't for me.

Life in the cabin wasn't too bad. At least we had a kitchen. There was no television reception so we drove into Cassville almost daily to rent movies and play them on the old VCR that we brought with us. We got discounts for volume and we were probably the video store's best customers for a couple of months.

Mark was constantly having surgery to remove scar tissue in an effort to improve his mobility. His arms were bent at an almost 45 degree angle and his little fingers were slowly curling into his palms. He couldn't raise his arms very high either and they had done a successful z-plasty under his arms that had the unexpected side effect of allowing him to stand flat footed. Before that he walked on his tiptoes. The doctors couldn't explain that one, but he was just happy to be able to walk better.

He had the most invasive and experimental surgery while we were in the cabins. The doctors decided to cut deeper into his arms and cover the open wounds with bovine tissue. This had never been done before and, at this point, Mark was up for anything. He just wanted to be able to use his arms better. The greatest risk was infection and we weren't exactly living in a sterile environment. I did what I could by changing our sheets and towels daily and keeping the cabin clean.

He also had to wear these arm brace contraptions designed to straighten his arms. He even had them for his fingers. For a while, his mobility was worse, but we managed to fight off any serious infections. A medical transport company came and picked him up for regular check-ups in Springfield. Mark also had physical therapy at the hospital in Cassville. After everything, Mark only has about a 55 degree extension in both arms and his pinky fingers are curled up. His doctors even advised that they be removed in order to allow him to do more, like put his hands into his pockets. He considered it, but decided against it.

It was sometime in June, almost a year after the fire, when they finally filed charges against Mark. We were living in the motel cabin and Ali was visiting us for the weekend. We found out when two Cassville police officers knocked on the cabin door around 11:00 at night. First they asked if Ali was there and told us that her mother was waiting at the police station to pick her up. They lead her to a waiting car after she grabbed her dad and started sobbing uncontrollably. She wouldn't let go of him and the police officer had to forcibly peel her off of him and drag her to the car. It was very traumatic for her.

They didn't put cuffs on Mark which was nice considering his physical state. He got in the other police car and we followed them to the police station. Evidently Leslie, Ali's mom, had learned of the charges and impending arrest and decided to play the heroic mother, to the rescue. The police only came and got Ali because Mark had another charge for a misdemeanor bad check from several years back that he had forgotten about. We were able to post bond immediately for a small amount and return to the cabin that night.

Greene County had filed 17 charges against Mark, including the old ones, but an arrest warrant had not been issued. We drove to Springfield on Monday and appeared in Judge Mountjoy's court. First we contacted Bobby Litton from Pre-trial Services who was supervising me and asked him to appear with us and offer to supervise Mark as well. It worked and Mark did a book and release after leaving court. It would be four long years before Mark's case was settled. I was off of probation before he was ever convicted.

I don't know if it was the police showing up at the cabin that tipped off the motel owners, or if it was just part of living in a small town, but we were suddenly evicted. They said it was because our animals had infested the cabin with fleas. Our animals did not have fleas, so I'm assuming we became undesirable tenants. The plan was for us to move into my brother's house in Monett whenever the Cassville house was finished and they moved in there. This was still a few weeks from happening, so we had to find somewhere else that would take four people, a cat and a dog, and let us pay by the week.

Our next temporary home was the Townhouse Hotel in Cassville. The problem was that they would not allow us to have the cat there. Ellie had to go. First we tried to find her a new home. I contacted some of my former co-patients from Lafayette House as well as some old friends from Cassville. No luck! We ran out of time and had to make a decision. Mark and I took her to a nice neighborhood and let her go. She was a beautiful cat, well taken care of, and we still imagine that someone took her in and she lived a very happy life.

Meanwhile, life at the hotel was rough. There was three of us plus a dog living there during the week, and Ali came almost every weekend. It was one room with two queen sized beds and a bathroom. There was a mini-fridge that we stocked with sandwich meat, cheese, condiments and milk. Bread and cereal rounded out our diet for the next three weeks. Not ideal, but at least we weren't starving. We brought a spare television from our storage unit and hooked it up for the kids. Mark had a headset that he could use to listen to one television and drown out whatever they were watching. I preferred to stay by the pool during the day, when I wasn't working, and lost myself in sleep or a book when I was not. And we longed for a place to call our own.

That day finally came in August. The house was finished and my brother and his family moved in leaving us their house in Monett. My brother's house payments were about $600 but he rented it to my mom for $1,000 a month. He told her it was because we were living there. I guess he was afraid we would burn it down cooking meth. I just couldn't believe that he would gouge his own mother like that, but I guess he had his reasons. She eventually bought the house and let us live there for several years. I sent her money to help with the rent a few times, but she told me to stop it, that she didn't want it and she wanted me to save my money to get back on my feet. Like I said, I owe her so much. I will definitely take care of her when she needs me to. She will never go to a nursing home as long as I am alive.

So we finally had a home and we did everything we could to make it our own. We made improvements like stripping wallpaper, painting, putting down wood floors and updating one of the bathrooms. The goal was for mom to make a profit when we moved out and she sold it. I moved out in 2012 when I finished school and got my job at Ozark Correctional Center in Fordland. I moved a couple blocks from where my daughter lived with her dad so that she could go back and forth easily and have full access to both of her parents. It worked out well because she moved in with me full time within a couple of months. Since I had both of my children living under my roof full-time, I truly felt that I had a home, because a home is filled with the people you love.

WORKING FOR A LIVING

Finding employment with several felonies can be difficult, but not impossible. Having child support enforcement come after you with garnishments did not help either. But I was able to find jobs and stayed employed most of the time, although I lost some of them for these very reasons.

As I said, my first job was cleaning condos in Branson. Not fun, but it helped out. My next move was to go to Penmac and find temporary work. My first Penmac job was at Miracle in the rotor room. It was a huge room with giant rotors that they poured plastic into to make molds for their various products. It was extremely hot in there and it was hard work. My problem came when they realized that I had no upper body strength, which was required to operate the power tools that opened and closed the molds. I lasted two weeks and was let go.

My next job was at Hydro Aluminum in Cassville. It's a factory that manufactures windows and doors. I had not done well at Miracle, so it was scary for me, but I acclimated and even came to excel at it. They eventually moved me to the doors department where we were paid more money. It was harder work and we worked longer hours, but that meant overtime and overtime meant more money.

After six months, they offered me full-time employment which would have meant more money and benefits. Unfortunately, one day the owner walked in, pulled me aside and told me that they had rescinded the offer. They found out about my pending felonies. So, I was unemployed again.

The next time I went into Penmac they told me that the Chamber of Commerce was looking for someone as their office worker and asked for a resume to fax to them. I was excited about this and quickly pulled together a resume and applied for the job. The interview went well, although I embellished the truth a bit when I told them that I was proficient at QuickBooks, which was required. I had used QuickBooks in my business, but only to write checks and track payroll.

It was at this time that I started abusing alcohol. My luck in the employment arena contributed to my depression and sense of worthlessness, so I was not in a place to take on a challenging office job. I remember going home for lunch on several occasions and consuming my then signature drink of vodka and lemonade, then going back to work. This did not help my overall job performance.

I recall one embarrassing moment when I was asked to meet the director at the Monett elementary school for the opening of the new playground. I asked her where the school was. I forgot that I had told her about my young daughter who was in grade school. She assumed that I would know where her school was, so she was confused. I believe I made up some excuse about my husband handling the school stuff. She didn't know about my felonies and the fact that my daughter did not live with me. I was mortified and I don't think she bought it.

If she was only suspicious at that point, she became sure something was up when she received a garnishment order from DCSE for child support for my daughter. I was behind on my payments, and they weren't willing to wait for me to catch up. It wasn't long after this that I was let go.

My next job was in Republic as an overnight desk clerk at the American Inn. After a few months there, once again, they received a garnishment order and I was abruptly fired. I knew at this point that something had to change. I couldn't go on searching for, obtaining, and then losing jobs due to my past. This is when I decided to go back to school.

Even though I was in school, working toward a better future, I still had to earn money so I could help pay the bills. I spent a few months drinking and feeling sorry for myself. I was even continuing to drink as I started that first semester of college. I remember a time or two carrying a pint or half pint of vodka in my back pack and taking surreptitious sips from it in the bathroom in Hill Hall. It's quite embarrassing when I look back on it now.

We had some student loan money to live on so I wasn't overly anxious to try my hand in the world of work again, but, when summer came, it became an imperative. I began putting in applications in earnest sometime in June. As my frustration grew and my expectations fell, I finally sat down with a phone book and started calling gas stations and fast food restaurants—any place that might be hiring.

To my surprise and delight, a call to Subway in Wal-Mart landed me a job. Tara, the manager, answered the phone and when I asked if they were hiring, she said yes. I told her a little about myself and she said "You're hired. Call me tomorrow and I'll tell you when you start." I was shocked. I'd never landed a job over the phone before. It was too easy.

The next day I called her back and she told me what I needed to wear as my uniform—black or khaki pants and non-skid shoes. Shirts and aprons would be supplied and I could fill out an application and W-4's when I got there to train. My first day was July 4, 2007.

Even though I had worked in the food industry before, it was scary at first. My introverted nature had taken hold of me by this time due to my many screw ups and that damned shame and guilt. I had also only been sober about six weeks, so my mind was not yet clear.

It's not that I couldn't do my job. I had grown up with a mother who worked many years in the food industry and she had instilled in me the values and work ethic that goes with it. In fact Tara seemed to be amazed at how thoroughly I did my job, especially closing the store. She wasn't used to new hires that actually did everything on the closing list and left the store clean and ready for the openers.

The problem was that I did not know how to talk to people anymore. I was the oldest person working there yet I felt intimidated and overwhelmed by my much younger coworkers, not to mention the customers. I was also told that I needed to smile and be friendlier. People who know me now wouldn't recognize me. At the very least, they would probably rush me to the hospital or to see a counselor because I truly was a shell of a person with no light in her eyes.

Eventually, the light began to return. My mind cleared, my self-confidence improved, and I began to function intentionally instead of on auto-pilot. I began to make friends with the ladies at work, but I did not yet feel close enough to them to tell them my story.

Tara gave me more responsibilities at the store like placing the weekly order and making up the schedule. She was only 19 and attending college at Crowder in Cassville. It was a little weird having a manager who was so young, but I was surrounded by young people, some still in high school. Tara had had a difficult childhood and was much more mature than other girls her age. Audrey, another coworker, was also 19 but we joked that she was 19 going on 40. Looking back, I see that I had some pretty great role models who eventually became really good friends.

I hadn't even been there a year when Tara decided to move on from Subway and asked me if I would be interested in applying for the manager's position. She had spoken to the district manager and she thought I would be good, too. I told her that I would, but had to confess to her that I had a criminal record involving drugs. Tara was shocked when I told her the whole story. She said she would talk to Christie about it but didn't think I would be eligible because of it. She was right. They hired someone else.

My mother likes to quote the statistic that if you hire a recovering addict who has been clean for at least one year, you have a much lower chance of having problems with that employee than you would if you hired someone who has never had a problem with alcohol or other drugs. The next several months played that fact out at Subway. The first manager that they hired cheated the time clock and stole entire deposits. I don't know if she was using substances, but she definitely was acting like a criminal addict.

The next manager that they hired was a nightmare. She had a drinking problem, an ex-husband who was abusing drugs, and three sons who like to steal, drink and do drugs as well. One week, she called in because her sons stole her money and her car and ran away. She had no way to get to work and she was trying to find them. Five days later the Chicago police department found her car and her youngest son who was abandoned by her two older sons.

She also liked to come in the store drunk at night to visit with whoever was closing. One night I was there and she started throwing potato chip bags across the store to get my attention. All of this was caught on camera of course and her trauma and drama was eventually too much for the district manager to handle so she was let go.

It was at this point that the owner decided that my criminal record could be overlooked and I was hired to manage the store. I tell my clients at the prison that it is very possible to get hired and promoted within an organization for a very simple reason. In four years, I never once called in sick. I almost always said I would come in to cover a shift when asked, and I was never late, usually at least 15 minutes early. Good help is hard to find, and if you can do these three things, you have a great chance at success.

Being promoted, along with my return to school, was one of the first accomplishments that truly shored up my personal foundation and gave me the confidence to push forward and rebuild my life. I took on the challenge wholeheartedly and with an ambition to be the best manager in their franchise. I did this by hiring the best employees, many of them recovering addicts who were trying to rebuild their own lives. We had the cleanest store with the friendliest "sandwich artists" as we were called. I made it my mission to learn the name of every one of my regular customers so that I could greet them by name.

I shared my food cost bonus with the other employees acknowledging that I couldn't earn a bonus without their help. I worked long days, sometimes lasting 12 hours. Admittedly, this allowed me to put in my 35 hour per week minimum in a few days while I attended Missouri State on the others.

This was a time of healing for me in a place that I felt comfortable, competent and respected. I made some good friends who I still consider friends, although we mostly see each other only on Facebook now. I still recommend it as a place to find work for those whose past may not be squeaky clean.

There are opportunities out there. It wasn't easy for me, but the point is to keep trying. Keep going. If you can get past the rejections, you will find someplace that welcomes you despite your troubled past and allows you to rebuild your self-esteem and self-confidence so that you can continue to rebuild your life.

NON-TRADITIONAL STUDENT

The decision to go back to school didn't feel like my own. I mean, I already had a degree in Professional Writing. It took me eight years to get that one with dropping out several times, going to cosmetology school, and running away from my problems. How was going back to college going to help me to rebuild my life?

I didn't see how my degree in writing was going to get me anywhere either. It hadn't so far. The only jobs I was landing were menial and definitely didn't require a bachelor's degree. And face it, I couldn't keep those for long what with my garnishments and criminal charges. After I lost the hotel night desk job, I got really discouraged, but Mark suggested that I go back to school.

I didn't know what career or degree to pursue so he suggested substance abuse counselor. Even though I didn't feel passionate about it, actually, I didn't feel anything at all, I agreed because it was someplace to start. I thought it was a bit trite—the addict becoming the substance abuse counselor—and I hate being trite.

Somewhere along the way I fought the substance abuse counselor title and tried to get my master's in Professional Writing. I lasted only several weeks before I dropped out. My mind wasn't ready and I don't think that that's what the universe had in mind for me. I finally relented and enrolled in the bachelor's degree program in Psychology.

It really wasn't as easy as all that, just enrolling. I found that I had to jump through some new hoops when I went back. On the Missouri State University application, they asked if I had ever been convicted of a felony. Boy had I? Try nine! It's understandable that the administration wanted to have a little talk with me, look me in the eye, and see if it was going to be safe having me roaming free over their campus, interacting with innocent young people.

So one day in the fall of 2006 I went to the university and met with the Director of Academic Affairs. As I recall, he was a very nice man. I was extremely nervous and embarrassed about the whole thing. He asked me several probing questions about my convictions (they were convictions by this time) as well as my life since then. I don't remember what I said, but, evidently I allayed his fears and he allowed me to register and enroll in classes. I started in January of 2007.

When you choose a major, you must also choose a minor. It was hard enough figuring out what my major was going to be and when asked to choose a minor, I was stymied. It takes 18 hours in an academic area to obtain a minor and I already had nine in history, so I initially went with a history minor. It was halfway through that first semester that I decided that was a mistake. History is hard. The tests were all "blue book" (essay) which involves a lot of writing and an ability to remember lots of specific dates and events in history. No multiple-choice or fill-in-the-blank questions here.

I wound up dropping my history classes and reassessing the situation. I'm not sure when the obvious answer came to me, but I eventually settled on Criminology. I say obvious because my life has been filled with criminal justice. My father and brother were both in the field; we owned a business at one point that provided private probation services to a few different counties in southwest Missouri; and, I spent a lot of time experiencing the other side of the coin as a criminal offender. In fact, I was on probation. How perfect is that?

As I stated previously, I was drinking my first semester in college. It all started with the infamous ice storm of 2007 when Mark suggested we pick up a 12-pack. We were bored and I had no self-control. Boredom is an addict's worst enemy. Or at least it was mine. I don't know how I did it, but I managed to get straight A's that semester. I only took nine hours per semester in my undergrad. I could have taken more that spring because I wasn't working, but I was drinking and drinking takes up a lot of your time when you're an addict.

After the night of May 21st, I quit drinking and soon got that job at Subway. This was the time that the sun started to rise. The dark night of my addiction and criminality lasted for several years, but I soon began to see a new future for myself. That vision was a vision of hope for something better—something better than the self-pity and shame that had engulfed me for so long.

This was the best time in my marriage, too. Mark and I were both students working toward new futures, our kids were proud of us, and we had recently begun the fight to bring Ali, his daughter, into our home. That came with its own set of challenges, but we were feeling like a real, stable family. We were also active in our recovery programs, but I'll say more about that in the next chapter.

I've never been an athlete, involved in organized sports, or competitive on any kind of playing field. But when it comes to academics, I am extremely competitive. Maybe it's not competitive with others as much as it is with myself. I get a great sense of accomplishment when I excel. We all need to have that feeling in our lives and, for me, it happened when I brought home A's.

Most people dread taking tests. They get anxious and worried, fearing failure. I, on the other hand, am excited by the challenge. I study with fervor committing myself to hours in front of the books and notes. I once calculated that for every test, I spent approximately 20 hours preparing. This included reading the materials and taking notes, as well as organizing my class notes and handouts in a logical order. Then I would read through it all, over and over, until it played out like a movie in my mind. I don't have a photographic memory, but if I look at something enough times, reading it to myself and out loud, I can actually see the printed words on the page.

A lot of people don't know that writing, seeing, hearing, and saying information engages multiple senses allowing information to be memorized more easily. I guess it's not "easy" per se, but it works. And the joy I got calling my husband after every test to tell him what

I scored was exhilarating. He was very supportive, but looking back, it must have been annoying at times. I remember one time when I studied really hard for a Psychology of Addiction test. I knew every important point about Motivational Interviewing that you could ask. When the teacher passed out the test, it was ridiculously easy. I was pissed. Who gets pissed off about an easy test? I do. I like getting A's, but I also like to feel like I earned them or it steals my joy.

In preparing for my eventual career in substance abuse counseling, I sought out classes that specifically had to do with this topic. There were only two, the one mentioned above, and Substance Abuse Interventions, offered by the Sociology Department. I was able to get that one to count toward my Criminology minor. Through my choices in class projects, I was able to do lots of research and emphasis on substance abuse. Every project I took on had something to do with it, whether it was Adolescent Drug Courts, Motivational Interviewing, or 12 Step Programs. It was a way to create my own degree of sorts.

Taking only nine credit hours per semester drug out my undergraduate work for over three years, but as I neared time to graduate I began to think, "What's next?" Maybe I liked school a little too much, or maybe it was because my mother was pushing me to go further. She still is, but that's another story. I had almost settled on pursuing a Master's Degree in Counseling from the Counseling Department across the quad, when my statistics teacher pulled me aside after class and talked to me out of it.

She told me I would be bored. I don't know how accurate her assessment was, but I took it to heart. She encouraged me to pursue a Master's in Clinical Psychology. I had already researched this and decided that there was no way I could get into this program. They receive about 60 applications each year and only choose nine applicants. They also required experience in research and a really high score on the Graduate Record Exam, or GRE. I took a practice GRE and only scored a 940. I would need something closer to 1200 to pass their standards.

So, I decided to beef up my school resume by volunteering to assist with the research being done in the Greene County Drug Court. I don't remember exactly what it was about, but each week I would go and interview new Drug Court inductees and ask if they would like to participate in the research. If so, I administered a few assessment instruments and obtained their agreements to take follow-up assessments throughout their programs. I enjoyed it somewhat, but the anger and frustration I felt each week when I saw some of them being put into jail for the weekend, or several days, was too much for me.

I had been in that same jail and seen so many women come in there without their medications and witnessed them decompensating until they were no longer functioning at all. I saw them losing weight, slipping into deep depressions, or even becoming psychotic. At that time, there was a limited pharmacy available and the only psychiatric meds I saw prescribed were Prozac and Haldol. And it could take several days to be seen and eventually actually get the medications, so my assumption was the worst case scenario. I don't know if I was correct, but my imagination took me to a dark place. Eventually, I made up an excuse about having to work early on those afternoons, and excused myself from the research activity. I was there long enough to get the experience though, and I put it on my application for the Master's program.

Meanwhile, I bought a GRE study kit from Barnes & Noble and crammed for the exam. I took the vocabulary cards to work and memorized them between customers. My son helped me with the math part which I scored an embarrassing 16% on, but I figured that if I scored high enough on the areas that I had a chance on, it would all even out. And it did. I took the test and got a score of 1160 with a 4 on the essay portion. It was close enough.

During the winter break, I wrote my personal essay. As usual, my life was an open book and I opened it for everyone on the committee to see. At that point I was 44 years-old, a recovering meth addict/meth cook, and convicted felon with charges ranging from Child

Endangerment to Manufacturing. I'm sure the entire committee was scratching their heads. I was also a straight A student with a decent GRE score, research experience and an intense drive to not only make my life better, but the lives of others who still suffered. It helped that I had a degree in Professional Writing and the skills to convey all of this to them with passion and clarity.

I don't know what I would have done had they not accepted me because I didn't apply anywhere else and I had put all my eggs in one basket, so to speak. But they did accept me and, that fall, I joined eight other, much younger, students as the new Master's in Clinical Psychology Class of 2012 of Missouri State University.

At the same time, my husband and I split up due to differences of opinion on parenting. I had started on a new journey, a greater challenge, but without the support and love that I had come to depend on. I was broken-hearted, but determined to succeed. I was also very close at this point to getting my daughter back, so my family was broken up, yet about to be put back together. It was a bittersweet time in my life.

In the Master's program I didn't have the luxury of just taking nine hours at a time. This program was unique in that it required us to take 12 hours each semester, plus nine during the summer so that we would all graduate together at the end of the two years. Nine hours is considered full-time in graduate school and this is one of the hardest programs on campus. So, taking 12 hours was extremely challenging. I continued to manage the Subway and studied more than I had ever studied in my life.

Of course, for me, getting anything but A's was unthinkable, so when I got two B's during that first year, I was devastated. It was too much for me. Working 35 hours a week at Subway, being on call all the time when my employees didn't show up or called in sick, made me curse out loud every time my phone rang or I got a text. Getting a C in this program will get you kicked out. So I applied for a teaching assistantship that paid for my school, plus gave me a stipend to live on. This was my excuse and way out. I got the assistantship and stepped down as manager until the fall semester started when I quit. It was a wonderful opportunity and I found that I was born to teach.

I taught two sections of "The Psychology of Personal Growth" to undergrads each semester. It was very rewarding and I never felt more alive than when I was up there teaching a class full of college students. That is until I taught a trailer full of offenders all dressed in grey. But that was in my future. Most of these students were there because they had to fill a Social Sciences requirement and they had heard that this class was not too bad. Some were on their way to Psychology majors or careers in the field, but most just wanted to get those three credit hours and never take a psychology class again. My future students in the prison were there because they had heard about my classes and wanted to learn about something other than relapse prevention. They had hope for a different future, or at least wanted to have hope. That is where my real joy came into the picture.

I finished my classes with my cohort in May of 2012 and was blessed to get the job working for Gateway at Ozark Correctional Center on May 18, 2012. It took me another six months to finish my seminar paper and present it before my committee. It was called "Readiness to Change: Improving Treatment Outcomes for the Reluctant Client." Of course it was, like all of my other projects, about substance abuse treatment.

I received my diploma in the mail in January of 2013. It was one of the proudest days of my life. My mother still pressures me to continue my education but I'm 53 now and I owe enough in student loans to choke a horse. And I don't think any more letters after my name will help me in my career, even if it would be Ph.D. If I did enter a doctoral program it would probably be one in Positive Psychology. That has come to be the focus of my studies and what I teach to my clients. I've come to believe that understanding what well-being is and how to create it in your life will do far more to keep you clean and sober than knowing about relapse triggers or someone's theories on relapse prevention.

There was a downside to graduating. I no longer had that report card to make me feel accomplished. My grades were validation that I was intelligent, competent and worthwhile. I needed a new outlet or platform to prove myself upon and that outlet came in the form of my new career. I still took tests. I had to take the National Counselor's Exam to become a Licensed Professional Counselor (LPC). And I took the exam to become a Certified Reciprocal Alcohol Drug Counselor (CRADC), and recently a Certified Reciprocal Advanced Alcohol Drug Counselor (CRAADC). I guess I found a way to keep getting a report card and it comes in the form of letters after my name which also includes Medication Assisted Recovery Specialist (MARS) and SATOP Qualified Professional (SQP). Now that there are more letters after my name than in it, I think I'll give it a break.

12 STEPPIN'

My first Narcotics Anonymous meeting outside of jail, or N.A., as we call it, was in Joplin during my 28-day stay in rehab. We would pile in a minivan a few times a week and go to a local meeting, or sometimes people would come to Lafayette House and hold a meeting for us there. Some of them were speaker meetings where someone with some serious time in recovery would come and tell their stories. In N.A., serious clean time could mean five years while, I later learned, Alcoholics Anonymous, or A.A., had people with serious clean time equaling 20 or 30 years.

Meetings were awkward and unfamiliar at first. It usually is for the newcomer. You walk into a room filled with people, most of whom know each other, and you feel out of place—like you don't belong. If you're lucky, there is a greeter there who is warm and friendly and tries to make you feel at home. The 12th Step is "Having had a spiritual awakening as a result of these steps, we tried to carry this message to addicts, and to practice these principles in all our affairs." Part of carrying the message and practicing the principles is to be of service and you learn that the newcomer is the most important person at the meeting.

The fifth Tradition states "Each group has but one primary purpose—to carry the message to the addict who still suffers." The newcomer is the one who still suffers and, as such, must be welcomed and embraced in order to give them the best possible chance of recovery. I was still suffering and I suffered for a long time after those initial meetings while I was in treatment. I don't remember specific names or if I was "greeted" officially, but I do remember getting lots of hugs and many recovering addicts trying to make me feel welcome.

I don't remember sharing much that first month. Maybe it was because I knew I wouldn't be going to those meetings again what with living in Cassville and all. I wasn't ready to open up to people I would never see again. Looking back, that was the perfect time to open up. They couldn't judge me any harsher than I was judging myself. And I'd never see them again, so why not? I had certainly heard some horror stories from them, yet, no matter how bad their stories were, they never felt as bad as mine.

When I completed Phase 1 of treatment, I moved to my parents' house in Cassville. I didn't seek out meetings at first. In fact, the first time it came up was at my father's funeral in January. A friend of mine from high school was there and he knew my story. Hell, it seemed like everyone did. He asked me if I had been to a meeting and I told him "no." He was new in recovery from an addiction to alcohol. He had started his own A.A. meeting and gave me some information about starting my own N.A. group. There was a meeting in Cassville, but it was having some problems and he said I wouldn't like it. Groups often split up just like churches when differences of opinion crop up about how the meetings should be run. I think that's what happened to the Cassville group.

Mark and I ordered some materials from the corporate office but never acted on it. We were really busy trying to survive at the time. When we moved to Monett, we went to the only N.A. meeting there and were really disappointed. The first time we went, there were four of us there. The second meeting there was only three. We didn't venture far from home to try to find something, but went to a couple of Aurora meetings. I'm not sure why we never went back.

This was about the same time that Mark met Cindy, the pastor's wife from New Site Baptist Church. They went to school together at Crowder and she invited us to go to their church. Wanting to create a "normal" family, we decided to go. Mark had never had any religious upbringing and he was really trying to make a connection with a God of his understanding. So we started going there every Sunday.

Mark became friends with Aaron, the pastor, and eventually the subject of Celebrate Recovery came up. They had a group that met every Thursday night at the church. It was still small and Aaron was hoping that Mark could help him to build its membership. So Thursday nights at Celebrate Recovery became our routine. It started at 6:00 with a dinner then the main group met at 6:30. The main group was more of a church service than anything. There was preaching and singing.

At 7:00 we broke up into small groups that were organized by gender and addiction or vice. I, of course, went to the women's substance abuse group. It was usually pretty small. Many of those ladies whom I knew were drug addicts chose to go to the "A to Z" group which supposedly covered everything else. One group was for relationship addicts. It was between the two as far as stigma is concerned. It was frustrating for me to see so many women in denial and everyone accepting it. There was even one lady who sang with the band during the large group that was obviously high on pills most weeks.

I don't want to sound like I'm bashing Celebrate Recovery. I'm just conveying what my experience was. I think it has been a Godsend to many people and has helped them with a strong spiritual, no religious, foundation where Jesus Christ is your Higher Power. As with N.A. or A.A., there are people there for the wrong reasons. In N.A., it may be to get a paper signed, or look good for court, or even hook up or get drugs. I guess those reasons abound in all 12-step programs.

I appreciated the fellowship of the dinners and getting to know so many truly good people. Really, the real problem was that Jesus is not my Higher Power and if you are going to be a hypocrite, don't do it in His name. Yes, I went to church there every Sunday, but I didn't do it because I truly believed the dogma of the Baptist church. I did it because I wanted us to be a family. I also went to Celebrate Recovery and became the small group leader, because I wanted us to be a family.

We chose to make the additional commitment to do step work on Sunday nights. Working the steps in Celebrate Recovery was serious business. They have booklets published for each of the steps and it is pretty intense to work them as a group. I went through it twice, leading the second time, and got a lot out of it.

About two years into our membership at New Site, Aaron asked Mark to head up starting a Celebrate Recovery group in Cassville on Tuesday nights. That was a lot of work, but he took to the challenge wholeheartedly. In fact, he still leads that group, as far as I know. He moved to Cassville when we divorced and Aaron gave him the church van to drive. His payment was to pick people up for church on Sundays, as well as for the Celebrate Recovery meetings. It's safe to say that he got a lot out of this program.

After Mark left, Logan and I started trying to find an N.A. group that we could belong to. We went to the Cassville group several times and were lucky that his sponsor, Jim, had started a group in Monett. The Monett group is called Vision of Hope which is the title of a reading from the meditation book for NA—Just for Today. Jim was trying to find a name for the group and he opened the book randomly and that is what he saw. It fits.

Logan started going there and he told me how much he enjoyed it, so I started going. It was a small group at first, maybe a dozen people each week, but it began to grow. Each time I went back, I felt closer and closer to the people who went there. Some came and went, while others stayed for the long-haul. They became like family to me and as we grew closer, my faith in 12-step programs grew as well.

Logan really got into it and began to leave early to go make coffee and visit with the members before the meeting. After I got unsupervised visitation with my daughter, she started going with us. She REALLY loved it. She and I became the unofficial coffee makers when she was staying with us. We would set up the tables with candy and the laminated reading materials. Her favorite part was that everyone knew that Michaela got to read the last card at the close of the meeting.

It's weird to think that an N.A. meeting would be quality time with your family, but my daughter remembers it as exactly that. She even talks about going back down there because she misses her N.A. family. We went to Vision of Hope campouts, barbecues and bonfires, not to mention a great Halloween party one year. Right before I left for Springfield, I held a barbecue and bonfire at my house. Now that's trust and it's what family does—fellowship.

I tried my hand at being a sponsor, but I wasn't very good at it. I think I had too much already on my plate. I had a couple of sponsors, but either I wasn't a very good sponsee or they weren't good sponsors. Whatever the reason, it all turned out okay. I still had women call me and I acted as a sponsor of sorts. Mostly they needed to talk when they were about to use. They always asked me how I stopped myself. I always told them that I just take a walk down that road, all the way to the end, and see where it would lead. That helps me to say "no" every time.

I went to a few meetings after I moved to Springfield, mostly for my son, but I haven't been in years. I'm still "12 Steppin'" but now I do it through my job. A popular saying in N.A. and A.A. is "You keep what you have by giving it away." That means sharing your experience, strength and hope with those who still suffer. I am blessed in that I get to do that every day I go to work. Not many people are that lucky and I feel truly blessed.

LIFE IS GOOD

When my academic advisor at MSU called to tell me that they were looking for substance abuse counselors at Ozark Correctional Center I thought, "Great, but they'll never hire me. I'm a convicted felon, many times over." I had tried to get an internship with the county jail and was turned away because of it. Why would a state prison allow me inside their walls? I expressed my reservations to him, but he urged me to call anyway. So I did.

Linda, the Clinical Supervisor, was happy to hear from me. They were in desperate need of help and I was more than qualified. It was so nice hearing someone express such excitement about having me work for her company. I hated to shoot down her expectations with the bad news about my criminal background. I decided I should tell her before she got too excited.

To my surprise, she wasn't concerned. I thought she must not understand what I was saying, so I laid it all out, all the felonies in all the gory detail. She asked if I was still on probation and I told her "no," that I was released two years early back in April of 2009. She asked how long I had been clean and I told her that it had been almost eight years. She then gave me instructions on how to apply online and told me that I would hear from her soon.

I interviewed for the job and was happy that they called me back for a second interview. I didn't realize until I got there that the second interview really meant that they wanted to hire me. When I tried to get through the sally port, I was directed to go directly to the training building instead. I was confused until the C.O. told me that I was supposed to go do a urinalysis. He explained that this usually meant that I was hired, as long as I passed the urinalysis. I wasn't concerned about that and gladly went my merry way.

My official hire date was May 18, 2012 but my first day on the job was June 4th. I remember feeling so blessed to be able to work with this population (addict offenders) that I almost felt giddy as I walked through the gates that day. I've been here almost four years now and continue to feel blessed and excited to go to work each morning.

I started on the evening shift that ran 12:00 noon to 8:30 pm. I was on the 1B treatment team. 1B was the wing designation in the housing unit—housing unit 1, B wing—and it's how we used to refer to them. Since that time, we've moved away from the housing unit identification to "family" names. Each wing chose a family name, 5 core values with symbols to represent each value, and created a vision statement and family crest that represents their ideals. That wing is now known as The Believers. There is also The Lion Hearts, The Guardians and The Incredibles in Housing Unit 1. In Housing Unit 2 we have The Bravehearts, The Legends and The Freedom families. I was privileged to head up these fundamental changes to the program.

Gateway Foundation Corrections is the company that has the contract to provide substance abuse treatment at O.C.C., as well as many other sites in Missouri. At this writing, they are in Illinois, Texas, Wyoming, and New Jersey. It is a modified Therapeutic Community. I have found that those in the treatment field have very strong opinions about therapeutic communities. They seem to either strongly support the efficacy of this model, or scoff at it. I didn't have an opinion one way or another but, through seeing the statistics on the success of those who leave O.C.C., I am now a believer.

The best part about working here is the leadership and the vision that has allowed us to be pioneers in the field of substance abuse treatment. There are a few things that stand out, specifically the quarterly festivals, the collegiate model, and Castles in the Sky. They all teach the clients that you can have fun sober, you can be successful in college and you can change your thoughts to help you to create the life you've always dreamed of. Our program director has tried very hard to incorporate elements of successful treatment into our program. He knows that self-determination creates "buy-in" and you have to buy in to the program in order to achieve success.

My favorite part of all this was the opportunity to create my own classes. When the collegiate model started, we were given this option along with teaching the basics of treatment that include the old standbys like relapse prevention, the psychopharmacology of addiction, and motivation to change classes. I believe that these are necessary and valuable classes, but my own experience and belief is that you will never maintain your sobriety until you build a life worth staying sober for. So I created my own classes that became quite popular.

My first class was "Living with Intention." This is a class about the law of attraction. The clients watch the film "The Secret" by Rhonda Byrne and practice all of the methods of manifesting the life that they truly want. They practice gratitude journaling, random acts of kindness, visualization, affirmations and much more. I think their favorite project during the 12 week class is doing vision boards. Considering their limited resources for materials, some of the vision boards that they create are amazing and they are very proud of them. The best part of this class is when I'm walking down Main Street and guys will call out to me about their successes using the law of attraction. I love it when they say, "I'm living with intention, Ms. Faber!"

The second class I created was really a revamp of the yoga class they already had in existence. Prior to my taking it over, the clients weren't actually doing any yoga. The staff facilitator was a male who was very intelligent and had a huge curriculum about yoga including its history and philosophical roots. I renamed the class "The Principles and Practice of Yoga" and made sure we had plenty of yoga mats. I plucked one part out of the curriculum, "The Yoga Sutra" by Putanjali, and broke it down into five lessons that they do every other week. Each class consists of 35 minutes of yoga and 15 minutes of meditation. I know that the meditation is their favorite part, but they all learn a healthy respect for the physical aspect of yoga. "Yoga is not for weenies" is what I saw time after time in their written assignments.

The third class that I created was "The Pursuit of Happiness" which is based on Martin Seligman's theories and book called "Flourish." It all started when I watched Ed Deiner's movie "Happy." It struck a chord with me as I realized that most of these guys are pursuing happiness through extrinsic rewards like money, status and image. The movie goes all over the world and shows what all of the happiest people on the planet have in common, which are all intrinsic rewards like loving relationships, positive experiences and volunteering. I teach them the PERMA model of well-being which includes positive emotions, engagement, healthy relationships, meaning and achievement. They also complete a character strengths survey and get a printout of their character strengths that encourages them to love themselves for the good things that they are instead of constantly being beat over the head with their character defects.

The fourth class that I created is called "Nutritional Healing." I have always been interested in nutrition, supplements and fitness. I have read a lot about these things and have practiced much of what I preach. When the director asked if someone could create a nutrition class, I was totally onboard. It started as a six week class, but I soon realized that I had too much information to cram it all into six hours, so I changed it up and it is now 12 weeks. In it, I show the movies "Forks Over Knives" and "Sweet Suicide." One is about the health benefits of a whole-food, plant-based diet and the other is about the evils of sugar. The rest of the class is lecture materials based on Dr. Joseph Mercola's book "Effortless Healing." It's all cutting edge material based on the most recent scientific research and the clients absolutely love this class.

I would be lying if I said I was a great counselor. I'm not. I'm adequate. This is probably because my passion lies in teaching. I taught other classes at O.C.C., some of them spur of the moment covering for absent facilitators, and others that I signed up for. Even those that I initially dreaded teaching, I enjoyed because it's who I am. I've never been afraid to speak in front of others. Teaching at MSU was the scariest experience for me, at least the first couple of times. And it was rewarding, not because of the experience itself, but because it prepared me for teaching in a prison. There is no comparison. The college kids were alright, but they were really just trying to fulfill a humanities requirement, while the "prisoners" chose my classes because they truly want to learn something and better themselves and their futures. At least most of them do.

So, when I was promoted to Clinical Supervisor not long ago, the one thing that gave me pause was turning over my classes, my babies, to another counselor to teach. I was not only giving up the experience of teaching this material that was near and dear to my heart, but I was entrusting its care and fidelity to someone who might not have the same passion that I do. Luckily, I was able to find counselors who became invested and excited about my classes and took them on. I am very happy that my contribution to the curriculum will carry on, although I have been approached by some who have begged me to come back to teach them because they are taking these classes for the second time and it just isn't the same. It's difficult to put down all of the knowledge that I have about these topics in a written curriculum because so much of it is in my head. I think they just miss my stories and illustrations.

I have also learned to let go of the experience and process it as something that happened to me that I cannot carry forward. If the classes morph into something else, then I have to trust the Universe to make them something even better. I am on a new path now in a new position with new responsibilities. I am finally able to utilize my organization and problem-solving abilities in a way that can help even more than my past client caseload. I am helping Gateway to meet its contractual obligations by auditing and observing and "fixing" issues when they are found.

I get to arrange for free aftercare for several clients each month saving each one hundreds of dollars. That feels awesome! My sense of what is moral and ethical and just plain "right" is guiding me in my efforts to see that all clients are treated with respect and receive the treatment they came here for. In a way, I feel as if I am an advocate for all of the clients while I also help the counselors to be the best that they can be. It's only been a few months, but, so far, the counselors have been very supportive of what I have been doing. I think they know that I have no hidden agenda and I just want our mission of "No More Victims" to be carried out with success. I know that the counselors must be successful in their jobs and feel empowered in order to fully develop as professionals.

I feel so blessed to be working where I am, doing the job that I do. Not many people are afforded the opportunity to do something meaningful with their work lives. They don't wake up each day excited for what the day will bring. I think about my job when I'm not there, but it's not with dread or worry. It's with anticipation of the next thing I get to do, the next person I get to help, the next big project I get to take on. And the thing is, if my life hadn't taken me down the dark path I traveled, I would not be equipped with the knowledge, skills and empathy that have made me so successful here.

My life at O.C.C. is not my only professional life. I have a consulting business called Vision of Hope, LLC. I work in the evenings and on weekends providing services to Christian County Drug Court, the Missouri Substance Abuse Traffic Offenders Program, the Alternatives Alcohol Minor Awareness Program, and, the Alternatives Batterer Intervention Program. I designed and implemented the last one from the ground up from Policies and Procedures to curriculum and credentialing. In fact, it was the first credentialed program in Southwest Missouri and currently has 33 clients. The best part of my "second job" is that I am able to continue to teach, which makes me very happy.

CLASS DISMISSED

Have I said what I started out to say? Have I conveyed the message that this book was intended to convey? The title says it all—"Vision of Hope: Rebuilding a Life Destroyed by Drugs and Alcohol." My goal was to give hope to those who still suffer and clarity to those with loved ones who still suffer. I didn't want to glorify or "gorify" the process of addiction. There are plenty of books out there that do that. And I didn't want anyone to get the idea that recovery is easy or even the same for everyone. I just wanted to tell my story so that others could see how I did it.

I hope that you come away from this book with an understanding of how insidious addiction is and how it can strike and destroy the lives of any one of us. I hope that you have had a peek inside at the lives of those confined in our criminal justice system and are able to see them as people, just like yourself. Yes, many of us turn to God or Jesus to save ourselves and are known as "jailhouse converts" but who doesn't turn to something greater than ourselves in times of extreme fear and dejection? Doesn't the cancer victim, the victim of violent crime, the victim of personal loss, also do the same?

I hope that you were able to see that this is not all that there is as I described the miracles and visitations of those who loved me during all of the madness and afterwards during my recovery. If you have lost a loved one to addiction or lost a loved one while you were in your addiction, just know that they are not gone. They see you in your grief and watch over you in your struggles. Time is linear for us, but for them, they can see far down the line to the place where you are healed, happy and prosperous. If you cannot see that for yourself right now, take comfort in the fact that they can.

We don't destroy our lives in a day, or a month, or even a year. The hardest thing for the criminal addict to understand is that it takes time to rebuild a life. But it can be done. It isn't easy and it isn't quick. The first thing you must have is a clear vision of what you want your life to be. It's that vision of hope that keeps you getting out of bed every morning and getting through the hard days. It's that vision of hope that helps you through the difficult phone calls to children you no longer have custody of and family members who don't really want to speak to you. It keeps you going as you look for a job when nobody wants to hire you and dare to hope for education and training that will allow you to provide a comfortable life for your family. It allows you to grieve for what and whom you have lost without staying stuck there in guilt, blame and denial.

It occurs to me that the greatest lesson I wish to convey is the lesson that I learned myself through teaching my classes. They are:

- Living with Intention: Create the life you want through intentional actions including practicing gratitude for what you have and appreciation for the people in your life. Rid yourself of fear of lack. Visualize and affirm the life you want and keep it ever in your sight.
- The Pursuit of Happiness: Remember that the best gift you can give your family and yourself is quality time. Find something engaging that creates a state of flow whether it's through your work or a hobby. Take the "mistakes" and other lessons in your life and create meaning from them. This usually happens by giving back and making the lives of others better in some way. And go after your dreams. Achieve something! It doesn't have to be something that would get you a Congressional Medal of Honor. It can just be that you are the best widget maker in the factory.
- Nutritional Healing: Drink more clean, pure water. Eat less meat. Eat more vegetables, especially organic and fermented

veggies. Allow yourself time to feel hungry. It's good for you. Exercise less but with more intensity. Minimize or cut out sugar in all its forms. Get more sun and walk barefoot in the grass.
- Principles and Practice of Yoga: Be strong, balanced, flexible and serene. Life throws drama and trauma at everyone. Be prepared and breathe through it. Find that quiet place where you can listen to the Universe and be assured that everything is going to be alright.

Be healthy. Be happy. Be prosperous. Love one another. Bless you!

Epilogue

"We're only as sick as our secrets" is a well-known 12-step phrase. This is how I had decided to start this chapter of the second printing of my book. I had decided that I couldn't in good conscience publish this book again without being totally honest about my life since its initial publication. It has a great ending. Did I really want to mess that up by inserting truth about the past six years that isn't exactly flattering? The answer is a resounding YES!

I wasn't shy about telling my truth before. Why should I start now? This epilogue is an important addition because readers need to know that no matter how long you've been clean and sober, it can be gone in the blink of an eye. In May of 2017, I relapsed on alcohol. After re-reading this book in preparing for its second publication, it became clear to me why it happened.

I admitted in my book that I never found a good sponsor, was no longer attending meetings, and attributed my sobriety to working the 12th step through direct services to clients. But what happens when that rewarding work is gone? January 1, 2017, I started my new job with Gateway Corrections in Dallas, Texas. I took a job implementing a new contract as the Clinical Director of a 350-bed inpatient treatment facility for Dallas Community Corrections. It came with a new title and a big raise.

What I hadn't counted on was the stress, frustration, loneliness, and lack of direct client contact, which brings me joy and keeps me sober. It was the most miserable 10 ½ months of my professional life. The only glimpses of joy were when I introduced Castles in the Sky and began teaching it to the clients. I also introduced and organized quarterly festivals, which the clients loved. At times, we were short-staffed, and I had a caseload which included teaching some classes and facilitating group therapy. But this only served to put more on my already overflowing plate and led to crippling stress.

One day, after having a breakdown on a bench outside, with several witnesses, my program manager called me and told me to take off and go somewhere. She told me to not come back until Tuesday. So I did. I packed up and went to Port Aransas for a few days. I got a motel, went to the island, and laid on the beach for a couple of days. On the last day, while walking to the ferry, I went by a frozen cocktail hut and saw several people drinking and having a good time. I stood there arguing with myself for a while, then finally ordered a frozen marguerita.

It was wonderful and I soon began to feel its effect on my brain. After 10 years of sobriety, it didn't take much. I went back to my motel, went to sleep, got up the next day and drove home. I tried not to think about it. But then I had another stressful day and stopped and picked up a bottle of wine on the way home. I did that often until I finally got a job in Oregon and moved to be with my family back west.

I did alright for several months while I lived with family and did Crisis work on a weird schedule. There were long days without much sleep, followed by several days off in a row. It was physically tough at my age, I was living in Washington and driving 40 minutes to Oregon to work. I'm not saying that I didn't drink at all during this time, but it was hit and miss, and I wasn't drinking to excess. I can see now that I was probably doing alright because I was helping people in crisis which is necessary for me to feel stable.

Then I was offered a promotion, with a huge raise, a new title, and an impossible job description. Sound familiar? I was to manage four different programs (intensive services) that serve the highest needs clients. They created this job just for me. Coworkers asked how in the world I was going to be able to do this. I said "I don't know. But I'll give 'er Hell trying." Concurrently, I bought a house and started dating a narcissistic sociopath who loved to drink. This was the summer of 2018.

Without dragging this story out too much, I'll just say that it was a recipe for disaster. By the summer of 2020, I was miserable. I was drinking vodka straight out of the bottle; doing terrible at my job which I hated; feeling stuck in an emotionally abusive relationship and hating myself. On August 20, 2020, I packed up my stuff and my family came and took me back to my house where my son and his family were living.

Covid didn't help as I worked from home a lot, so I was free to keep drinking unrestrained. My family knew some but not how bad it had become. This went on until May of 2021 when I was doing yardwork and broke my sacrum. The pain was excruciating. I went to the ER twice and they did an x-ray and then a CT scan but didn't see anything. So I would go home, but the pain kept getting worse.

On May 25, the pain was so bad, I couldn't walk. I called my sister and asked her to take me back to the ER. On the way there, I broke down and told my sister about my drinking. I poured out my heart about how unhappy I was and how I needed something to change immediately. She went in with me and we told the doctor everything. They gave me medications to help with the withdrawal symptoms. They called a crisis worker to come talk to me and possibly get me placed, but that didn't work out.

They did an MRI and could see then that I had a bilateral fracture of my sacrum. The only cure is to lay down and stay down. I finished detoxing at my sister's house, laying on her couch. She waited on me and helped me to the bathroom and the bedroom because I couldn't really walk without help. I was on Tylenol 3's for a couple of weeks until I started to heal, and the pain diminished. Eventually I went and stayed with my mom and continued to heal, physically and emotionally.

I was off work for two months and went back in August with a new job title and a lower salary. I took the Clinical Supervisor position over one of the programs I had been managing. We serve mentally ill adults with psychotic disorders. Our goal is to keep them out of a higher level of care. We help them to remain stable in their homes in the community. And there you have my 12th step, back in my life.

In November, I started doing online mental health teletherapy for a well-known company. I do this 15-20 hours a week, in addition to my "day job." I get to help people with addictions, anxiety, depression, and an assortment of other life problems. I have become a much better therapist. I've met people all over the world and obtained an entirely new world view.

I know. You're asking, "But what about meetings and a sponsor?" In my early recovery I was going to online AA meetings. I got a lot out of it. The meetings I went to were in places all over the state of Washington, except in the town I'm from. I was too embarrassed and fresh in my recovery to let anyone know, aside from my family. I also read books.

One made a huge impression on me. It's by Holly Whitaker and it's called "Quit Like a Woman." There is a lot of good information in it. But one thing stuck with me. She says that where women get into trouble is when we question our decision to never drink again. It's not that we need to take inventory and admit our wrongs. Women are constantly taking inventory and wallowing in what we did wrong. What women need to do, she says, is NEVER QUESTION THE DECISION (N.Q.T.D.). In fact, she has a tattoo—nqtd--on her arm. I now have nqtd inside my right wrist written in red ink. I see it every day, multiple times a day, and it reminds me that I CANNOT question the decision to never drink again.

I think the lesson for me was to know myself better. Know what keeps me sober. Know what it takes to feel joy in life. Know to never chase titles and money. Know that helping people is my life's calling and if I'm not doing that, I'm walking on thin ice.

www.ingramcontent.com/pod-product-compliance
Lightning Source LLC
Chambersburg PA
CBHW071905070526
44583CB00016B/1859